AJ C5

P9-ELX-741

Salse di Pomodoro

Salse di Pomodoro

MAKING THE GREAT TOMATO SAUCES OF ITALY

JULIA DELLA CROCE

PHOTOGRAPHY BY ELLEN SILVERMAN

CHRONICLE BOOKS

SAN FRANCISCO

Dedication

For my dear little daughters, Gabriella Leah and Celina Raffaella.

Text and recipes copyright © 1996 by Julia della Croce.
Photographs copyright © 1996 by Ellen Silverman.
All rights reserved. No part of this book may be reproduced in any form
without written permission from the publisher.

Library of Congress Cataloging-in-Publication Data

Della Croce, Julia.
    Salse di pomodoro : making the great tomato sauces of Italy / by Julia della Croce.
        p.   cm.
    Includes index.
    ISBN 0-8118-0930-7
    1. Cookery (Tomatoes) 2. Sauces. 3. Cookery, Italian. I. Title.
    TX803. T6D45   1996
    641.6'5642—dc20   95-32802
                                              CIP

Designed by Laura Lovett.
Food Styling by Sally Schneider.
Prop Styling by Fritz Karch.
Printed in Hong Kong.

Distributed in Canada by Raincoast Books
8680 Cambie St., Vancouver, B.C. V6P 6M9

10 9 8 7 6 5 4 3 2 1

Chronicle Books
275 Fifth Street
San Francisco, CA 94103

Contents

Acknowledgments

I WOULD LIKE TO THANK all those who helped create this book: my mother, Giustina Ghisu della Croce, for always standing by with her infallable palate, and for her help with testing recipes; Alexander Barakov for proofreading; Victor Gil for computer assistance; Flavia Destefanis, Anna Amendolara Nurse, Paula Wolfert, Dahlia Carmel, Marcia Jean, Lucky Lee, the "Tomato Lady," Anna Teresa Callen and Elio Serrá for their contributions to my research; and Nancy Q. Keefe, Jenna Holst, and Justine and Charles Kadoche for tasting with discrimination. Thanks also to the Alltrista Corporation for their assistance with technical questions regarding canning and preserving, to Pamela Paizs of Happy Hovel Foods in Yelm, Washington, for advice on preserving, and to Diane Barrett of the University of California at Davis for providing a greater scientific understanding of the tomato.

To my editor, Bill LeBlond, and my agent, Judith Weber, who together fostered the idea of this book; to my associate editor, Leslie Jonath, who has smoothed out many wrinkles in the editorial process; and to my copy editor, Sharon Silva, whose skill and intelligence shine through this book, I here express my very great gratitude.

I am grateful to others whom I do not know personally, but whose works have added to my knowledge and understanding of the subject. My sources include *Columbus Menu*, by Stefano Milioni; *The Healing Foods*, by Patricia Hausman and Judith Benn Hurley (Dell, 1989); *Heinerman's Encyclopedia of Fruits, Vegetables and Herbs*, by John Heinerman (Avery, 1988); *Foods That Heal*, by Bernard Jense, M.D. (Avery, 1993); *Food: An Authoritative and Visual History and Dictionary of the Foods of the World*, by Waverly Root (Simon and Schuster, 1980); *La scienza in cucina e l'arte di mangiar bene*, by Pellegrino Artusi (1891, reprinted by Giunti Marzocco, 1960); *Gastronomia parmese* (Ferrutius, Parma, 1952); "Through the Kitchen Window: Italy Seen from the Pages of a Nineteenth Century Cookbook," by Kyle M. Phillips III, *The Journal of Gastronomy*, Vol. 5, No. 4, spring 1990; and "The Arrival of the Tomato in Spain and Italy: Early Recipes," by Rudolf Grewe, *The Journal of Gastronomy*, Vol. 3, No. 2, summer 1987.

Introduction

NOWADAYS, THE FLAVORS OF THE ITALIAN TABLE are known throughout the world. Surely, the tomato and, specifically, the sauce that is made from it, characterizes Italian cooking more than any other ingredient. Sadly, however, tomato sauce has generally not traveled well. Look at the tomato sauces found in many American restaurants, in bottles on supermarket shelves, and in the pages of cookbooks written outside of Italy. They are often misconceived. Should green pepper, dried oregano flakes, garlic powder, sweeteners, or the likes of raspberries ever appear in a proper Italian tomato sauce? Why are tomato sauces prepared outside of Italy so often overcooked, or even scorched? Why is it commonly thought that the sauce should be simmered for hours until every hint of tomato sweetness is cooked out of it?

The result is that the ubiquitous miscooked sauce that for decades has covered Italian dishes in America has obscured a true understanding of authentic Italian cooking on this side of the Atlantic. Thus, when Italians visit America, it is scarcely to be wondered at that they are unfamiliar with so much of the red-covered fare that they are told is "Italian."

In the beginning of my career as a food writer, I was dismayed by this state of affairs and decided to sidestep the subject of tomato sauce altogether. Along with other Italian cookbook authors and culinary teachers, I sought to spread the word that authentic Italian cooking is not limited to tomato sauce–covered dishes.

As the decades unfolded, one new dish or product after another was introduced to an American population enamoured of Italian food, and

Americans were given a broader view of the Italian kitchen. But when I look around and see what Italian dishes people are cooking at home, those based on tomato sauce still predominate. Everyone loves them and they always will.

In the pursuit of chic food and ever "new" Italian imports, many Italian food aficionados threw the baby out with the bath water. Now that many Americans have begun to discover the great diversity in authentic Italian cooking, it is time to vindicate the tomato and tomato sauce.

There is nothing inherently offensive about tomato sauce. Indeed, no other sauce can universally juxtapose itself with other ingredients so successfully. We all know about its affinity for pasta. But its uses should by no means be limited to the contents of the pasta pot. Throughout Italy, even in Naples, where the image of *sugo di pomodoro* atop a pile of steaming spaghetti has become a motif in the region's folklore, literature, and song, tomato sauces have myriad uses. A simple tomato sauce is the basis for bean stews, rice dishes, and fish soups. Tomato sauces that include sausages, meat, or mushrooms are spread between layers of *polenta*, or even folded into the cooking pot just before the polenta is taken off the stove. Such flavorful tomato sauces turn a simple white *risotto* into a main course.

Tomato sauces can moisten a meat loaf or a hamburger brilliantly, pep up a batch of meatballs, enhance fish and chicken dishes, and transform a poached egg. A cold, uncooked tomato sauce made with fruity olive oil is a revelation with breaded veal cutlets, and can convert a mere slice of toasted bread into an appealing *antipasto*. Zesty *pizzaiola*, the Neapolitan tomato sauce redolent of garlic and oregano, was invented to rescue an inferior cut of beef, and no leftover bones from a roast ever had better treatment than those simmered in a liquorous sauce of tomatoes, red wine, and rosemary.

When speaking about a person who is temperamental, the Sicilians say, "*Cambia sempre come la salsa,*" which means, "He is always different, like a sauce." A Frenchman would no doubt conjecture that the author of the aphorism was thinking of *béchamel* and *béarnaise* besides *ragù* and tomato sauce when this bit of brilliance came to his lips, but an Italian would realize that he could have easily been contemplating only the countless varieties of *salsa di pomodoro*. Outside of Italy, Italian food aficionados talk about the quest for the quintessential "spaghetti sauce." The point is that there are tomato sauces *ad infinitum*: There are raw ones and cooked ones, sweet ones and racy ones; tomato sauces that taste of the sea and tomato sauces that deliver the prodigious flavors of the vegetable world. Whether combined with pungent olives, heady wild mushrooms, peppery rocket (arugula), or sweet, fragrant basil, tomatoes are welcome. Even among basic tomato sauces there is great variety in ingredients and cooking methods: Some are buttery, velvety, and refined; others are chunky and fruity; some are relatively complex and others are astonishingly simple.

This little book will go a long way toward showing how delicious, varied, and creative Italian tomato sauces really are. Most of the recipes in these pages are for making sauces the way the Italians make them, that is, for making a tomato taste like a tomato. Except for *ragù*, sauces that include meat, Italian tomato sauces are cooked quickly. Few spices are used and, outside of the chapter on *ragù*, few require long lists of ingredients. The Italians refer to their cuisine as *cucina sana*, literally, the "healthy kitchen." I prefer to interpret the phrase to mean the "sane kitchen," because in my mind it is an oasis in today's mad world of fast foods, junk foods, and convenience foods. Italian cuisine is founded above all else on fresh and quality ingredients, and on its simple and honest preparation. Tomato sauce allows us to enhance a multitude of dishes without the use of cream or of sauces made from lengthy reductions and stocks.

I hope these pages will help to provide a better understanding of how to cook what is surely Italy's most popular sauce, and to inspire ideas for preparing it in new ways.

The History of the Tomato and the Sauce in Italy

IN ORDER TO APPRECIATE THE SAUCE, it is necessary to understand the tomato, where it came from, and how it made its way into our lives. Probably no other plant has traveled as rocky a road to acceptance and universal appeal.

Although the tomato appeared in Italy in the middle of the sixteenth century, it was not accepted in Italian cooking until some three hundred years later. Numerous theories explain the transport of the tomato from the lower Andes to Italy, but the one that seems most plausible suggests that it was introduced by the Spanish through the kingdom of Naples, which was established in 1522, around the time explorers brought the tomato back to Europe. While the French appreciated the ornamental attributes of the small golden berry (Olivier de Serres, agronomist under Henry IV, writes that "they serve commonly to cover outhouses and arbors"), the Italians experimented with it both in the garden and in the kitchen. As a result, by 1700 the "golden apple" had evolved from a marble-sized berry into *Lycopersicum rubeo non striato*, a nonribbed red fruit closer in size and appearance to the plum tomato of today.

Yet it was considered unpalatable and even toxic in its early years. Thus in 1544, naturalist Petrus Matthiolus refers to the tomato as the *mala insana*, the "unhealthy apple." In his description, he says that it is eaten like an eggplant, "fried in oil with salt and pepper." Later, Castore Durante offers a similar recipe in his *Herbario nuovo*, published in Rome in 1585: "They are eaten the same way as eggplants, with pepper, salt, and oil, but give little and bad nourishment." References to the berry's ill-effects were echoed by others writing at the time. Pietro Antonio Michiel writes, "If I should eat this fruit, cut in slices in a pan with butter and oil, it would be injurious and harmful to me." Such references to the believed dangers of eating the tomato proliferate in England, France, and other countries of Europe. As a way of getting around this perceived toxicity, early recipe books recommended cooking tomatoes for three hours to make them safe to eat.

Despite the warnings, Italian cooks continued to experiment with the fruit. By the beginning of the eighteenth century, numerous references appeared for cooking tomatoes into a sauce. Among those writing on the subject was Padre Francesco Gaudentio, who stocked the larder for a Jesuit community in Rome. This expert recorded a recipe in 1705 for cooking tomatoes into a kind of stew with oil, salt, garlic, and wild mint. Another specialist, Antonio Latini, writes in *Lo scalco alla moderna* (the modern master of household), first issued in 1692, that the fruit (tomato) and the sauce made from it were beginning to make their debut in royal households. At right is one of Latini's sauces.

Rudolf Grewe, a scholar on the subject of the appearance of the tomato in Spain and Italy, points out that this early tomato sauce recipe bears a clear resemblance to the tomato sauces described by travelers and explorers in the New World. One Francisco Hernández, on a botanical expedition, reports that the native inhabitants of Mexico used the *tomatl* with chili in "a delicious dip sauce . . . which complements the flavor of almost all dishes and foods, and awakens a dull appetite." Another chronicler of New World Aztec culture, Bernardino de Sahagún, describes a dish offered by a food vendor in the market. "She . . . usually mixes the following: *ají* [hot capsicum pepper], [squash] seeds, tomatoes, green chilies, and large tomatoes, and other things that make the stews very tasty." Such accounts suggest that tomato sauces were commonplace in at least parts of the New World.

Despite the chill with which it was first received, no other post-Columbian food had as significant an impact on the everyday lives of

TOMATO SAUCE, SPANISH STYLE

Take half a dozen tomatoes that are ripe, and put them to roast in the embers, and when they are scorched, remove the skin diligently, and mince them finely with a knife. Add onions, minced finely, to discretion; hot chili peppers, also minced finely; and thyme in a small amount. After mixing everything together, adjust it with a little salt, oil, and vinegar. It is a very tasty sauce, both for boiled dishes or anything else.

DUMMENECA *(Sunday)*

As I entered the door, I smelled
the aroma of ragù.
So . . . Take care . . . Goodbye . . .
I am leaving . . . If I sit
I might not go . . .
I might wait
'til you sit at the table . . .
That's not right

I'm sure it is macaroni
I heard cracking
as I entered the door. Could it be?
If the kitchen is complete today with
brasciole, and meat.
No tomato paste: all fresh tomatoes
passed through a sieve . . .

A tomato skin is resting on your arm
like a blood stain . . . Permit me?
I will remove it! How fine
your skin feels . . . like silk,
slipping under my fingers . . .

You look especially beautiful this
morning.
Your face reflects fire . . .
You look more colorful.
I am sure it's the macaroni and ziti
that makes you so.

I am going . . . Goodbye!
If I sit, I might not leave . . .
I might wait
'til you sit at the table, waiting for
your kiss with the ragù flavor.

Italians. The tomato thrived in the Italian climate and soil; it was at home in a land that Italians describe as *cultura della verdura*, a "vegetable culture." The Italians eventually not only adopted the once-suspect fruit, but, in characteristic fashion, also transformed it into their own. (This penchant for adopting foreign influences is peculiarly Italian; in terms of food, it is particularly felicitous—witness how corn was transformed into *polenta*, potatoes into *gnocchi*.) Italian cooks developed recipes that merged New World ingredients with Old World techniques and tastes. What started out as an experiment among the *conoscenti*, and a vanity of chefs in royal households, became a passion that infiltrated the populace.

The tomato and the sauce became especially popular in Campania, in particular between Naples and Salerno, where some of the best tomatoes in the world are still cultivated. Mixed with *maccheroni*, the sauce transformed the subsistence diet of the massive plebian class, providing nourishment as well as flavor. Before tomato sauce, the *mangiamaccheroni*—"macaroni eaters"—as the Neapolitan rabble were called, dressed their pasta with pig's fat and grated cheese. Once housewives developed the sauce, *i maccheroni* became a joyful food. The popular passion that developed for the sauce and its Sunday variation with meat, *ragù*, is perhaps best illustrated in this spoof (at left), written in the Neapolitan dialect in 1932 by Rocco Galdieri, and reprinted in my book, *Pasta Classica*.

From Naples, the sauce spread to Sicily, where it was often combined with eggplant and other ingredients introduced by the island's Saracen invaders. In Apulia, *ragù* is made with lamb, because of the sheep that thrive in the mountainous southern regions. Even on the remote island of Sardinia, which until modern times typically resisted the influences absorbed by the mainland, the sauce emerged with its own regional accents; in a recipe unique to the island, saffron is added to the tomato sauce.

Generally in the south, sauces were simple and if there was meat, it presented itself in small quantities. In northern Italy, tomato sauce took on a refinement that reflected the comparatively rich cooking styles of more verdant regions. In accord with the northern climate and economy, sauces typically incorporated many kinds of meat—beef, pork, and chicken. They were initiated with butter; sometimes, even cream was added. A taste for the sweet was characteristic of the cuisine of the Italian Jews in whose tradition are found highly sweetened tomato sauces, or *salse di pomodoro agrodolci* (sweet and sour). In short, in virtually every region, the sauce seems to have merged with localized ingredients or traditions and evolved into distinctive recipes.

Differing climates between north and south also affected styles of cooking. Kyle M. Phillips III points out in a paper published in *The Journal of Gastronomy* that the tendency was to cook foods less in the south than in the north. For instance, a *ragù* in Emilia is cooked for four hours, in Tuscany it is cooked for some two hours, and in Sardinia for one hour.

Salse di pomodoro virtually revolutionized Italian cuisine. In his *Il cuoco galante* (the gallant cook), written in 1765 and the first real recipe book of Neapolitan cooking, Vincenzo Corrado calls it a "universal sauce . . . [that] can be used to flavor meats, fish, eggs, pastas, and vegetables." At the end of the nineteenth century when, as a result of the industrial revolution, dried pasta became a cheap food of the masses, the love affair between pasta and the tomato blossomed. The union resulted in a long and happy marriage of which the whole tribe of *salse, sughi*, and *ragù* are a result.

By 1891, when Pellegrino Artusi wrote *La scienza in cucina e l'arte di mangiar bene* (the science of cookery and the art of eating well), the first Italian cookbook that spoke of a national Italian cuisine, the tomato had clearly been adopted throughout Italy. The extent to which Italian cooks viewed its possibilities in the kitchen is perhaps best illustrated in one of Artusi's anecdotes:

There was a priest in a small village of Romagna who had the habit of putting his nose into everything and . . . into everyone's family affairs. He was, however, an honest man, and more good than bad came from his meddling, so he was left to do what he would; but the sharp populace baptized him "Don Pomodoro" to indicate that, just like the tomato, he could fit and be welcome everywhere; therefore, a good sauce from this fruit will always be an aid in the kitchen.

Fundamentals

Tomato Table of Equivalents & Conversions

Nutritional Value of Tomatoes

Making Sauces with Fresh Tomatoes
WHAT TYPES OF TOMATOES TO USE AND HOW TO
PREPARE THEM FOR SAUCES

Storing and Preserving Tomatoes
FREEZING, DRYING, AND HOME CANNING TOMATOES,
PURÉE, AND PASTE

Using Canned Tomatoes in Sauces
NATIONAL AND REGIONAL VARIATIONS,
VARIOUS CANNED TOMATO PRODUCTS

Cooking Techniques
QUICK COOKED OR LONG SIMMERED,
STRAINED VERSUS UNSTRAINED

TOMATO TABLE OF EQUIVALENTS
& CONVERSIONS

5 pounds fresh plum tomatoes yield approximately 6 cups peeled, seeded, chopped, and drained plum tomatoes

One 28-ounce can plum tomatoes in natural juices contains 2½ cups drained tomatoes

One 35-ounce can plum tomatoes in natural juices contains 3 cups drained tomatoes

One 28-ounce can crushed plum tomatoes contains 3 cups crushed tomatoes

2½ pounds fresh tomatoes yield approximately 2½ cups cooked tomatoes, including their juices

2½ pounds fresh, mature vine-ripened peeled plum tomatoes are equivalent to 2½ cups canned, peeled plum tomatoes in juice

2½ cups canned, peeled plum tomatoes packed in purée are equivalent to 2½ cups canned plum tomatoes plus 3 tablespoons tomato paste

One 6-ounce can tomato paste contains ¾ cup, or 12 tablespoons, paste

NUTRITIONAL VALUE OF TOMATOES

The vine-ripenend tomato is full of minerals and nutrients, and is high in vitamins A and C. Doctors recommend vine-ripened tomatoes to purify the liver and to remove toxins from the body, especially uric acid. It is well known that tomatoes are high in potassium, which helps kidneys to function and aids in controlling hypertension. Tomatoes are also helpful in dissolving fat that can clog arteries, and they make an effective poultice for relieving stagnant blood conditions and for healing sunburn, festering wounds, and sores. According to researchers at Harvard Medical School who tracked the diets of one thousand people during a period of five years, the chances of dying of cancer were lowest among those who ate tomatoes every week.

Approximately one-third of the vitamins in fresh tomatoes are lost during cooking, but the majority of the nutrients remain intact. Uncooked tomato sauces deliver maximum nutritional value, but cooked tomato sauces are also good sources of vitamins and minerals.

APPROXIMATE NUTRITIONAL VALUE IN ONE POUND
VINE-RIPENED TOMATOES

Calories	100	Iron	2.7 mg
Protein	4.5 g	Vitamin A	1,350 I.U.
Fat	9 g	Vitamin C	34 mg
Carbohydrates	17.7 g	Thiamin	0.23 mg
Calcium	50 mg	Riboflavin	0.15 mg
Phosphorous	123 mg	Niacin	3.2 mg
Potassium	350 mg	Ascorbic acid	102 mg

MAKING SAUCES WITH FRESH TOMATOES

*What Types of Tomatoes to Use and
How to Prepare Them for Sauces*
The most delicious tomato sauces are those made
with gloriously sweet vine-ripened Italian tomatoes.
I have lovely memories of growing such tomatoes
myself, even as a child, in my own little garden. It
was unthinkable to pick them until all of the green
deepened into the most vibrant fire-engine red. And
in any case, they didn't want to be picked until they
were ready to drop into my hand at the faintest
tickle of their warm dusty skin. The ambrosial snap
as the fruit fell from the vine was promise enough
that those tomatoes would burst into sweet, dripping lusciousness when I bit into them. They were
as good to eat as the ripe, sugary fruits that weighted
down peach-tree branches in late summer. And to
cook those sweet "golden apples," what more was
needed than to coddle them in a little warm sweet
butter or fragrant olive oil scented with a scrap of
basil? *That* was tomato sauce!

Such tomatoes are a dream in the cold climates
of America, but they can be grown where the summers are long and dry. The ideal environment for
good-tasting tomatoes is a hot one (the tomato plant
doesn't get going until the soil warms up to 65 degrees F or more, and nighttime temperatures start
passing the 50-degree-F mark), with a long growing
season of very hot, dry days and little rainfall (tomatoes
should be wilting before they are watered; frequent
watering produces weak roots and tasteless fruits).

Vine-ripened tomatoes may not always taste as
good as they look, however. I have brought the best
tomato seeds from Italy to plant in New York,
where summers can be torrid. I once produced a
crop of tomatoes that was stunning to look at, but
so lacking in flavor that it was virtually inedible.
There had been too much rainfall that summer and
the soil had not drained well.

Before buying fresh tomatoes, always taste first.
Don't despair of ever finding tomatoes good enough
for making sauce. Go to local farmers' markets and
taste, taste, taste. Tomatoes that are shipped long
distances are often disappointing, even if they look
beautiful. Because ripe tomatoes are fragile and
don't ship well, growers pick them before they are
ripe and mature them artificially with ethylene gas.
Those that are picked under these conditions have
not yet developed their vitamin content (vitamins
are present in tomatoes only in the last weeks of
ripening). Besides this, tomatoes traveling long distances can be dull tasting and mealy in texture by
the time they get to us. There are more and more
organic tomatoes grown locally nowadays, and they
can be very good. Cherry tomatoes are often very
sweet and are available year-round. While they are
tedious to seed and clean, they can be quite suitable
for sauces.

The ideal tomato variety for sauces is the plum
or Roma tomato, which is fleshy and contains fewer
seeds than other varieties. Because the plum tomato
contains less water, sauces made with it do not have
to be cooked as long to evaporate excess liquid, thus

the clear, fresh tomato taste is not simmered away. If you have found sweet, vine-ripened tomatoes of other varieties, they can be made into sauce successfully, although you may have to increase the quantity because they will most likely contain more water than plum tomatoes. If using other varieties, cut the tomatoes in half crosswise, or into quarters, if large, then squeeze out the juice and seeds before proceeding with your recipe. This way, excess water will be removed from the tomatoes before cooking, thereby reducing the time on the stove.

To prepare fresh tomatoes for sauces, it is necessary to first peel them and remove excess seeds. While many cooks do not insist on removing seeds, I find their slightly bitter taste and slippery texture unappealing. The easiest way to peel and seed tomatoes is to submerge them in rapidly boiling water for 30 to 45 seconds. Then drain the tomatoes and immediately plunge them into cold water. Blanching in this fashion will loosen their thin skins, which are then easily lifted off using a paring knife (do not keep the tomatoes in the boiling water longer, or they will begin to cook, and too much of the flesh will come off when you lift off their skin). Next, cut out the tough core portion. Cut the tomatoes into quarters lengthwise and, with your fingers, push out the excess seeds. Nonplum varieties have more seeds and a looser core section; with these tomatoes, the whole core section of seeds can be pushed out. Another method for peeling tomatoes is to hold them over a flame to loosen their skins, but I find this method too tedious.

STORING AND PRESERVING TOMATOES

Any fruit or vegetable tastes best when it is first picked, for at that moment it is at the height of its full flavor. Tomatoes are no exception. The longer they are stored, the more of their natural sugars, flavors, and nutrients they lose, so, if possible, pick and eat them at their peak of ripeness. Once cut, they should be eaten or cooked immediately as they oxidize quickly, and thus lose a great deal of their nutritional value. For sauces, tomatoes should be extremely ripe, even soft.

To store ripe tomatoes, keep them at room temperature in a basket that allows for air flow. The ideal temperature for tomatoes is 60 to 65 degrees F. They should never be refrigerated, for chilling arrests their flavor. If the temperature drops below 48 degrees F, the juices crystallize, thus altering their flavor permanently. Despite what many people say, bringing the tomatoes back to room temperature does not restore their flavor.

Freezing Tomatoes
Proper freezing preserves the flavor, nutritive value, and color of tomatoes and most other foods far better than any other preserving method. But because tomatoes have a high water content, their texture breaks down substantially once frozen. The result upon thawing is little fruit and a great deal of water. A way around this problem is to blanch the tomatoes first, which slows or stops the enzyme action that causes loss of flavor, color, and texture, and

then to parcook the peeled, seeded tomatoes to evaporate excess liquid before freezing. Plum tomato varieties, because of their comparatively low water content, are the best varieties for freezing. If the tomatoes are exceptional tasting when fresh, they are likely to make good sauces as long as they are frozen properly at their peak of flavor and freshness.

To prepare tomatoes for freezing, first immerse them in boiling water to blanch for 30 to 45 seconds. Then drain the tomatoes and immediately plunge them into cold water. Using a small paring knife, lift off their skins and cut out the tough core portions. Cut the tomatoes in quarters lengthwise and, using your fingers, push out the seeds. Chop them and place in a colander to drain off as much of their juices as possible. Place the chopped tomatoes in an uncovered saucepan and bring to a boil. Reduce to a simmer and cook over medium-low to medium heat until the excess liquid has evaporated, 20 to 25 minutes. Allow to cool completely and then freeze in a tightly capped container or a lock-top bag. Frozen tomatoes taste best if used within 3 months, but they will keep for up to 6 months. They should be thawed at room temperature before cooking. For sauces, cook the tomatoes as you would canned or fresh tomatoes. Because they have been previously cooked, they will need less time for evaporation, so adjust the cooking time accordingly.

Drying Tomatoes

Sun-dried tomatoes are unknown in the cuisines of many Italian regions. It is only in the south of Italy, where the climate provides perfect conditions for sun-drying, that these preserves are found. Various methods for drying are used. When the tomatoes are miniature, the whole plant is hung upside down under the sun, thus drying the tomatoes directly on the vine. Another method calls for salting them in the manner of salted capers. This is done with ripe plum tomatoes by first cutting them in half lengthwise and scraping out the seeds, and then laying the halves, covered with sea salt, on a clean grate or rack on a rooftop or other open-air surface until they are thoroughly dried. They are then layered with more sea salt and, perhaps, basil in large terra-cotta urns. The salt is rinsed off before the tomatoes are used.

Dried tomatoes are not considered appetizing when eaten whole, combined with pasta, or as part of an appetizer, a practice that has become popular in American restaurants. In Italy, they are cut up and typically added to stews, stuffings, sauces, and other dishes. Also, because Italian cooking is so strongly geared toward the seasons, dried tomatoes are used only when fresh ones are unavailable. Then they are combined with bottled or canned tomatoes for sauces, or made into a *pesto* with garlic and olive oil (like the one on page 83) for pasta or for adding to soups and stews and the like. When used to fortify tomato sauces, dried tomatoes are first finely chopped, playing a role similar to that of tomato paste.

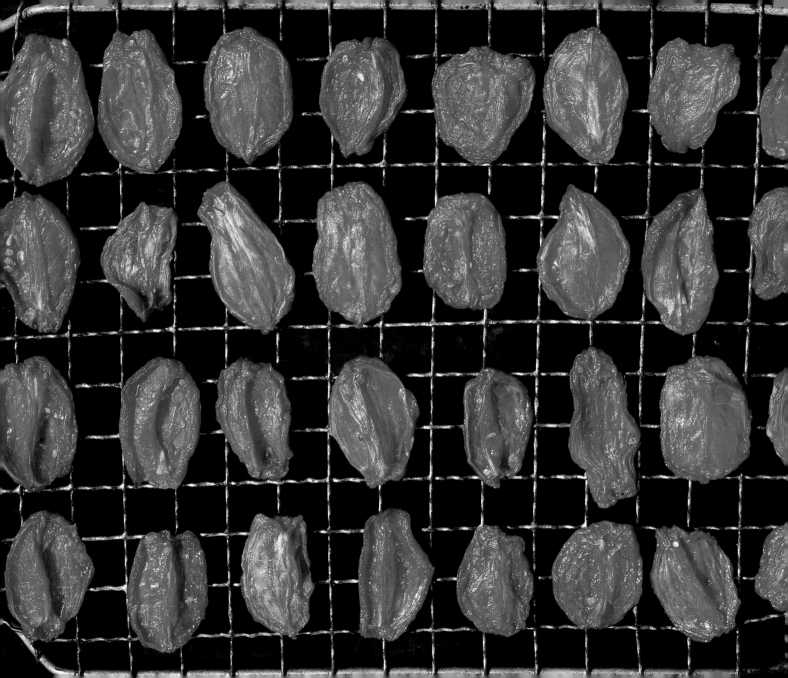

While the hot and dry southern Italian climate makes it possible to dry tomatoes in the sun, most of us are not able to duplicate these ideal conditions: long, dry summers of daily temperatures in excess of 90 degrees F, no air pollution, and the absence of insects. The best indoor method for dehydration is probably an electric dehydrator, which dries foods quickly, and therefore, economically, evenly, and thoroughly. We can, however, dry tomatoes in an oven in relatively small quantities.

If the tomato is not fleshy and sweet in its fresh state, it will produce something similar to shoe leather when dried. The only tomatoes worth drying are meaty plum tomatoes. They should be very ripe but unbruised, free of blemishes, and sweet.

Dry no more than 6 pounds of tomatoes at one time in a standard home oven. Blanch them in boiling water for 30 seconds, and then plunge them into cold water. Using a small, sharp knife, peel them and cut out their cores. (Blanching improves the flavor of the tomatoes when they are dried, so don't be tempted to eliminate this step.) Cut the tomatoes in half lengthwise and push out their seeds.

Preheat an oven to 160 degrees F. Select baking sheets that are at least 1½ inches narrower than the oven cavity to allow for proper circulation. Allow at least 2½ inches between the trays and 3 inches of headspace at the top of the oven. Arrange the tomatoes in a single layer on a wire mesh tray placed over a baking sheet. Brush lightly with olive oil on both sides. Bake for 6 to 8 hours until dry. Check the tomatoes every hour or so for uneven drying or scorching (discard any scorched tomatoes; they will have a strong, unpleasant flavor). Change the position of the trays periodically to ensure even drying. The best test for proper dryness is to weigh the tomatoes. If they weigh half of what they did when they were fresh, they are done. The tomatoes will still be quite moist and have a highly concentrated flavor. Such tomatoes would make excellent dried-tomato pesto (page 83). Place the tomatoes in freezer bags and freeze for up to 1 year.

The most interesting and thorough source of information for drying tomatoes and other vegetables in the sun, or in an oven or dehydrator, is the United States Department of Agriculture (USDA) Garden Bulletin No. 217, available through local cooperative extension agents. Because the booklet was written to help educate missionaries abroad on drying fresh produce, it is especially detailed on sun-drying tomatoes and storing them without refrigeration.

Dried tomatoes that are not preserved in oil must be soaked in boiling water to cover before using. The length of soaking depends on how thoroughly dried the tomatoes were. Home-dried ones may take as little as 5 minutes, while store-bought ones may take up to 15 minutes. The tomatoes should have a tender feel when they have soaked long enough. Drain and pat dry. Lay them on a baking sheet and slip them into an oven preheated to 250 degrees F for 10 minutes. Remove from the oven. At this point, the rehydrated tomatoes can be used immediately, refrigerated for up to 4 days,

frozen for up to 1 year, or packed into a jar and covered with olive oil. Covered in oil, rehydrated dried tomatoes will keep in the refrigerator for many months.

Home Canning Tomatoes, Purée, and Paste
It is wise to familiarize yourself with the latest methods for foolproof bacteria-free preserving, as such procedures are regularly updated. Good sources for canning safety are local cooperative extensions (these are organs of county governments nationwide), and the Alltrista Corporation, manufacturers of Ball Brand Home Canning Products (telephone: 800-240-3340). Alltrista publishes an excellent, inexpensive canning guide called the Ball Blue Book (Alltrista Corporation, Consumer Products Company, P.O. Box 2729, Muncie, Indiana 47307-0729).

The water-bath process for home canning is simple to do and requires little in the way of expensive equipment. But preserving is a science, so follow the method precisely to be sure that you have proceeded safely.

Whether preserving tomatoes whole or for purée or paste, only vine-ripened, sweet, bruise-, and disease-free tomatoes should be used. The tomatoes must be mature, at their peak of flavor and nutritional value, but they should not be overripe, because overripe tomatoes lose their acidity as they begin to deteriorate. Tomatoes from dead or frost-killed vines are not safe to can.

Home-Canned Tomatoes

Assuming that you begin with excellent-tasting vine-ripened tomatoes, these home-bottled tomatoes are good enough to use in uncooked tomato sauces (pages 42–62). While the peeled tomatoes can be bottled whole, I prefer to cut them into quarters before preserving them—no point in preserving unwanted seeds and excess liquid. The final yield will vary depending on the water content of the tomatoes (see Yield).

6 POUNDS FRESH, SWEET, MATURE VINE-RIPENED PLUM
  TOMATOES
4 TO 8 LARGE FRESH BASIL LEAVES
1/4 TEASPOON CITRIC ACID POWDER FOR EACH PINT JAR
4 PINT PRESERVING JARS WITH LIDS AND RINGS

Bring a kettle three-fourths full of water to a rapid boil. Meanwhile, inspect all the tomatoes carefully and reject any that are bruised, cut, or unripe. Wash them well in clear running water. Slip the tomatoes into the boiling water and blanch for 30 to 45 seconds after the water returns to a boil, or until the skins start to split. (If your kettle is not large enough to accommodate all of the tomatoes at once, do them in batches.) Do not leave the tomatoes in the boiling water once the skins split or they will begin to cook and too much of the flesh will come off when you lift off the skins. Using a slotted utensil, remove to a bowl of cold water to arrest the cooking. With a paring knife, lift off the skin of each tomato and carve out the core about 1/8 inch deep.

Cut the tomatoes in half crosswise and squeeze out the excess seeds; discard the seeds. Place the tomato halves in a colander over a bowl to drain for about 15 minutes, reserving the juices.

Select 4 pint preserving jars with rings and lids. Inspect the jars carefully; reject any that are scratched, cracked, or damaged in any way. Wash them and the lids and rings well with hot soapy water and rinse with hot water. Leave the jars in hot water until needed. Place the lids and rings in a saucepan filled with water and bring to a simmer (180 degrees F). Cover and remove from the heat; set aside until needed.

Working on a flat surface, fill the jars with the tomatoes, pressing gently to pack the tomatoes well enough to fill spaces. Insert 1 or 2 leaves of basil in each. Add enough of the captured juices to fill each jar to within 1/2 inch of the top. Using the long handle of a wooden spoon or a hard plastic "bubble-freer," poke any air bubbles in the tomatoes to burst them. Add more of the captured tomato juices if necessary to bring the tomatoes to within 1/2 inch of the top of the jar. Add 1/4 teaspoon citric acid to each jar; place it square in the center on top of the tomatoes. Using a clean, damp paper towel or cotton kitchen towel, thoroughly clean around the rim and threads of each jar. Transfer one lid at a time from the simmering water to the top of each jar. Screw on the rings evenly and securely, but don't over-tighten them by using a gadget or any instrument.

Select a water-bath canner with a tight-fitting lid. Fill it half full with hot but not boiling water.

Place the jars on a rack in the kettle. If you do not have a rack, use a clean, folded terry cloth kitchen towel to keep the jars off the bottom of the pot. The kettle should be large enough to accommodate the jars so that water circulates around them (that is, do not pack them tightly in the kettle), and deep enough to allow water to cover the jars by 2 inches. Allow 1 to 2 inches headspace to prevent the water from boiling over the kettle sides. Now pour in enough hot—not boiling—water to cover the jars by 2 inches. Place the cover on the kettle and do not remove it until the process is complete.

Bring the water to a boil over very high heat, then turn down to medium. Process the pint jars at a gentle but steady boil for 40 minutes (quart jars require 45 minutes) at altitudes under 1,000 feet above sea level (between 1,001 and 3,000 feet, add 5 minutes; between 3,001 and 6,000, add 10 minutes; between 6,001 and 8,000, add 15 minutes; between 8,001 and 10,000, add 20 minutes).

Turn off the heat and uncover the kettle. Using a jar lifter, transfer the jars to a rack (metal, wood, or heatproof plastic) or a wood surface or folded cotton kitchen towel to cool. Do not place them on a solid metal surface or in a draft. When the jars have cooled thoroughly, or before 24 hours have passed, check the lids for a good seal; they should be slightly concave and not push back when pressed. Label, date, and store in a cool, dry environment for up to 1 year. Once opened, store in the refrigerator for up to 4 days.

YIELD: Makes 3 or 4 pints. On the average, 12 pounds raw fresh tomatoes yield 8 pints canned tomatoes; 22 pounds will yield 7 quarts; 1 bushel (53 pounds) yields 18 to 20 quarts. Thus, approximately 2¾ pounds raw fresh tomatoes yield 1 quart.

Passato
TOMATO PURÉE

At the end of summer in Italy, wherever the climate supports good tomatoes, it is commonplace to see families "putting up" passato, thick tomato purée. The tomatoes are first washed, then passed through a passatutto, the equivalent of a food mill, to strain out the skins and the seeds. The liquid is simmered to thicken, and the resulting purée is transferred to bottles and jars that have been saved throughout the year solely for this ritual. Fresh basil is added to each bottle or jar, which is then capped and sterilized in huge kettles of boiling water.

As with canned tomatoes (see end of recipe), the yield will depend on the water content of the tomatoes.

5 POUNDS FRESH, SWEET, MATURE VINE-RIPENED PLUM TOMATOES
7 TO 14 LARGE FRESH BASIL LEAVES
¼ TEASPOON CITRIC ACID POWDER FOR EACH JAR

Sort through the tomatoes and discard any that are bruised, cut, or unripe. Wash them well in clear running water. Cut the tomatoes in half crosswise and squeeze out the excess juice and the seeds. Cut each half in half again and place them in a colander to allow liquid to drain off, about 15 minutes. Then use a potato masher to force out any additional juice.

Transfer the tomatoes to a nonstick (preferably) or heavy-bottomed pot and bring to a boil. Reduce the heat to medium and simmer, uncovered, at this pace until the tomatoes are reduced to a pulp. This should take approximately 30 minutes, but the time will vary greatly depending on the water content of the tomatoes. Stir the simmering tomatoes occasionally with a heatproof plastic or wooden spoon. The pot should remain uncovered at all times to evaporate as much of the water in the tomatoes as possible.

Remove the tomatoes from the heat. Position a food mill fitted with the disk with the smallest holes over a clean pot (preferably nonstick) and pass the tomatoes through it. (Be sure to use the finest-holed disk to prevent tomato seeds from being forced through the mill.)

Return the tomatoes to a boil and then reduce the heat until the tomatoes are at a gentle simmer. Cook, uncovered, over low or medium-low heat until a thick purée forms, about 1 hour (the tomatoes should be reduced by about one-half). Stir occasionally. The tomatoes should simmer gently but steadily.

Select 7 half-pint preserving jars with rings and lids. Inspect the jars carefully; reject any that are scratched, cracked, or damaged in any way.

Following the directions for Home-Canned Tomatoes (page 25), ready the jars, lids, and rings. Then, continuing to follow the directions, fill the jars and push in the basil, leaving $\frac{1}{4}$ inch headspace and using $\frac{1}{4}$ teaspoon citric acid powder per jar. Process half-pint jars for 30 minutes (pint jars require 35 minutes and quart jars require 40 minutes) at altitudes under 1,000 feet above sea level (between 1,001 and 3,000 feet, add 5 minutes; between 3,001 and 6,000, add 10 minutes; between 6,001 and 8,000, add 15 minutes; between 8,001 and 10,000, add 20 minutes).

Remove the jars from the canner, cool, and check for proper seals as for canned tomatoes (page 25). Store in a cool, dry environment for up to 1 year. Once opened, store tightly covered in the refrigerator for up to 4 days.

YIELD: Makes 6 or 7 half pints. Approximately 28 pounds raw fresh tomatoes are needed for 9 pints purée, 46 pounds for 7 quarts, and 1 bushel (53 pounds) yields 7 to 9 quarts. Thus, approximately $6\frac{1}{2}$ pounds raw fresh tomatoes yield 1 quart.

Concentrato di pomodoro (Estratto)
HOMEMADE TOMATO PASTE

Concentrato, or in Sicily, estratto, is tomato paste. It is used to add body, flavor, and color to many sauces and other dishes. If you have a large quantity of good, ripe tomatoes at the end of the summer, you may want to make concentrato, as many Italians do. Most likely it won't have the bitterness of some commerically canned tomato pastes, so sauces that call for the addition of paste will be sweeter and lighter.

In this method, the tomatoes are first cooked on the stove top to evaporate as much water as possible, and then transferred to an oven set at the lowest temperature for further long, slow evaporation. The USDA no longer recommends the water-bath preserving process for home canning of tomato paste because the density of the concentrate may not allow for the heat penetration necessary to kill all bacteria. The paste can be put into 4-ounce canning jars, however—much more practical than the commercial 6-ounce cans—and frozen for up to a year.

10 POUNDS FRESH, SWEET, MATURE VINE-RIPENED PLUM TOMATOES

Bring a large kettle three-fourths full of water to a rapid boil. Meanwhile, sort through the tomatoes and discard any that are bruised, cut, or unripe. Wash them well in clear running water. Slip the

tomatoes into the boiling water and blanch for 30 to 45 seconds after the water returns to the boil, or until the skins start to split. (If your kettle is not large enough to accommodate all of the tomatoes at once, do them in batches.) Do not keep the tomatoes in the boiling water once the skins split, or they will begin to cook, and too much of the flesh will come off when you lift off their skin.

Drain the tomatoes. When they are cool enough to handle, use a paring knife to lift off the skin of each tomato and to carve out the core about 1/8 inch deep. Cut the tomatoes in half crosswise and squeeze out the excess juice and the seeds. Cut each half in half again and place in a colander to allow excess water to drain off, about 15 minutes. Then use a potato masher to force out any additional juice.

Transfer the tomatoes to a nonstick (preferably) or heavy-bottomed pot and bring to a boil. Reduce the heat to medium and simmer, uncovered, at this pace until the tomatoes are reduced to a pulp. This should take approximately 30 minutes, but the time will vary greatly depending on the water content of the tomatoes. Stir the simmering tomatoes occasionally with a heatproof plastic or wooden spoon. Reduce the heat only if the tomatoes begin to boil rapidly after stirring. The pot should remain uncovered at all times to evaporate as much of the water in the tomatoes as possible.

Remove the tomatoes from the heat. Position a food mill fitted with the disk with the smallest

holes over a clean pot (preferably nonstick) and pass the tomatoes through it. (Be sure to use the finest-holed disk to prevent tomato seeds from being forced through the mill.)

Return the tomatoes to a boil, and then reduce the heat until the tomatoes are at a gentle boil. Cook over low or medium-low until very thick, about 2 hours. The tomatoes should boil steadily, forming bubbles on the surface that break immediately. Stir occasionally, especially at the end of the cooking time when the mixture is more likely to stick to the bottom of the pot. (The nonstick pot will allow you to dislodge easily any concentrate that has stuck to the pot bottom and sides.)

After 2 hours, transfer the tomato purée to a shallow baking dish and place it in an oven preheated to 200 to 250 degrees F. Leave the purée in the oven until it is very dense and has evaporated into a paste, 4 to 5 hours. Stir occasionally to prevent a crust from forming.

Remove the dish from the oven and transfer the paste to 4-ounce jars with tight-fitting lids (canning jars with lids and rings are good). Allow the jars to cool completely at room temperature, then label and freeze for up to 1 year. Once thawed, store in the refrigerator in a tightly capped container for up to 4 days, or pour in enough olive oil to cover the concentrate and store, refrigerated, for up to about 1 week.

YIELD: Makes approximately fourteen 4-ounce jars.

Using Canned Tomatoes in Sauces

National and Regional Variations

In sauces, good canned tomatoes are an excellent alternative to fresh tomatoes. Not all canned tomatoes are equal, however. Fruits of the Italian San Marzano plum variety, which are picked ripe at their peak of sweetness and flavor, are the best sauce tomatoes. Comparatively thin-skinned, meaty, and with less water and fewer seeds than other types, they are particularly suitable for use in sauces. Their lower water content allows for quicker cooking than other varieties, which means their clear tomato taste remains intact.

Imported Italian plum tomatoes are not easy to find, though. Since 1989, high tariffs have doubled and even tripled their price, forcing many companies (even whose labels bear an Italian logo) to base their operations in Turkey, Israel, Argentina, and other countries whose climates approximate Italian conditions. A few specialty brands are sold nationally, but they are not widely distributed. Some brands are only available in certain regions, while others are sold to supermarkets who then sell them under their own private labels. And finally, tomatoes will naturally vary in taste and texture from season to season, depending on the amount of rainfall and other climatic conditions. Thus, the only way to know what brands are best is to try several and judge for yourself.

Here are some things to look for when comparing various brands of canned tomatoes: The labels should list no additives or sugar. Tomatoes should be meaty and whole, not flabby and disintegrated. Fleshier tomatoes produce thicker sauces with more body than thin, watery ones. Nor should they be excessively seedy. Their flavor should be full-bodied and sweet, not overly acidic. Organic products are always preferable to those cultivated with the use of pesticides and other chemicals, so if you find the other criteria present in canned organic tomatoes, consider them a good buy. Notice that some brands have more tomatoes per can than others. For this reason, it is a good idea to measure canned tomatoes by the cup rather than by the weight of the can when following recipes (a 28-ounce can should yield 2½ cups drained tomatoes). Keep in mind that canned tomatoes should be used very soon after the can is opened. Because tomatoes oxidize very quickly, they lose a great deal of their mineral value once exposed to the air.

Various Canned Tomato Products

WHOLE TOMATOES IN NATURAL JUICES VERSUS TOMATOES PACKED IN PURÉE. Tomatoes packed in their own juices can sometimes be used interchangeably with tomatoes packed in purée. If it is only the tomatoes you are after because you intend to drain the juices (such as for Light Puréed Tomato Sauce, page 43), either type is suitable. But in sauces calling for tomatoes packed in purée, the purée is intended to thicken and bind (alternatively, you can add tomato paste to tomatoes packed in their own juices). In other sauces, such as Tomato Sauce,

Harlot Style, Hot Version (page 75), canned tomatoes packed in their natural juices are required because the ingredients of the sauce—capers, olives, large bits of garlic—must stand out as separate elements. The sauce is simmered long enough to evaporate the juices until the desired thick consistency forms.

CRUSHED TOMATOES. Precrushed tomatoes can be very convenient, eliminating the need to remove excess seeds and to chop, but their quality is sometimes unreliable. If you find a brand that is consistently thick and chunky instead of watery and thin, with good, sweet flavor and no sugar or other additives, stock up on it. As with canned whole tomatoes, measure crushed tomatoes by the cup rather than by the weight indicated on the can when following recipes (a 28 ounce can should yield 3 cups crushed tomatoes).

TOMATO "SAUCE." The highly strained tomato product called tomato sauce has limited use in the making of authentic Italian tomato sauces. It is not as thick as tomato purée; therefore it needs to be cooked an unnecessarily long time before the proper sauce consistency is reached. It also does not have the pleasant chunky texture of purée, which is what we are often after in rustic sauces. This sauce is useful for *polpettone* (meat loaf) or other baked or roasted meat dishes that call for what amounts to a tomato glaze, as it does not dry as readily as purée does in the oven.

TOMATO PURÉE. In Italian tomato sauces, tomato purée, or *passato*, is added to the *soffritto* (sautéed onion, garlic, carrot, celery, or what have you) in place of chopped tomatoes. *Passato* produces a consistent, smooth sauce that still retains some pulpiness (unlike the canned tomato sauce just discussed), while chopped or crushed tomatoes create a meaty consistency and robust texture.

TOMATO PASTE. In Italy, tomato paste is associated with winter sauces, as it is unnecessary to rely on tinned or preserved products when glorious fresh tomatoes are in season. While the hot, dry southern regions produce tomatoes of notorious flavor, Parma, in the region of Emilia, has also excelled in the cultivation of superior tomatoes. The same province seems to have been the birthplace of tomato paste, or *concentrato*, which was at one time called *conserva nera*, or "black conserve." The product that was described in 1811 by agronomist Filippo Re is the same one that is made today: "The tomato is used when it is fresh but in addition the juice is pressed from it and it is reduced to a solid consistency, so that it can be used . . . throughout the year."

The commercial tomato paste industry began in Parma in the beginning of the twentieth century. Some 250,000 tons of tomatoes are needed to make 35,000 tons of *concentrato. Doppio concentrato* (double concentrate) requires the same volume of tomatoes to produce approximately 32,000 tons, while *triplo concentrato* (triple concentrate) reduces the volume even farther.

Before the development of the canning industry, tomatoes were dried in the sun, and then, as recorded in *Gastronomia parmese* (1952), compressed into "loaves the color of dark mahogany, of the consistency of stucco, cylindrical in form, well oiled and wrapped in oiled paper. In winter it was . . . also eaten, spread on bread, by children." The making of tomato paste at home was one of the culinary traditions Italian immigrants transplanted to America. In *New Homes for Old*, published in 1921, sociologist Sophonisba Breckinridge describes the difficulties encountered by the Italian-born homemaker in America's urban tenements of the early twentieth century: "Tomato paste is made at home by drying the tomatoes in the open air. When an attempt is made to do this in almost any large city the tomatoes get not only sunshine, but the soot and dirt of the city."

Despite its importance in the larder, *concentrato* is used parsimoniously in Italian sauces. Its primary function is to thicken tomato sauces (while in soups, bean and lentil dishes, and meat sauces, it is used to add an intensity of color as well as flavor and thickness). It also adds acidity and depth to sauces made from canned tomatoes. Tomato paste is not meant to be used in sauces made with fresh tomatoes, as it obstructs the sugary clearness of the fresh fruit.

Many Italian recipes for sauces made with canned tomatoes don't call for tomato paste because Italian canned plum tomatoes are fleshy and immensely flavorful. The canned Italian-style tomatoes available in America now (see discussion on canned tomatoes on page 31) may not always be substantial enough to stand alone in a sauce; that is, some brands may be flabby and thin rather than fleshy, lacking in flavor, or too acidic. Adding a little paste will round out a sauce and bind it; it will impart a boost of flavor, a thicker texture, and more depth of color. Used in excess, however, tomato paste can destroy a good sauce, making it heavy and too acidic.

Tomato paste actually constitutes the entire tomato base of some sauces, such as Tomato Sauce with Squid on page 110, and Tomato Sauce with Onion and Rosemary on page 82. In the squid sauce, the natural sweetness of the shellfish and the generous amount of broth it leeches into the sauce dilute the intensity of the tomato concentrate. Red wine expands the flavor. In the sauce with onion and rosemary, the large volume of onion actually wants the sharpness of concentrated tomato to balance excess sweetness.

Tomato paste sold in cans is very cheap, despite the enormous quantity of fresh tomatoes required to make it. As with other tomato products, flavor varies from brand to brand, so experiment to find a concentrate that has sweetness as well as pleasing acidity. *Concentrato* sold in tubes is often less acidic, but also significantly more expensive because it is imported. A recipe appears on page 28 for making *concentrato* at home.

Once opened, a can of tomato paste can be stored in a freezer in small freezer-safe containers. If you think you will have use for the excess tomato

paste within about a week, keep it in a refrigerator in a covered glass or plastic container with enough olive oil to cover.

COOKING TECHNIQUES

Making sauce with canned tomatoes is a straightforward process, but there are a few techniques to keep in mind. First, remove the excess seeds by pushing them out with your fingers. This step may be unnecessary if the tomatoes are not very seedy, and many Italian cooks are not adamant about this, but I find that the seeds are bitter and have an unappealing texture and appearance. Don't rinse the tomatoes under running water as you work, as this causes tasty juices to be washed away. There is no need to be fanatical about removing every seed; just expel the excess. To crush the tomatoes evenly, use your hands, a fork, or better, a potato masher. After the sauce is cooked, add a tablespoon or two of butter or extra-virgin olive oil to round out the flavor and improve consistency.

There are two basic approaches to cooking sauces. In the first, a *battuto* initiates the sauce: garlic or onion, or a combination of chopped raw vegetables and aromatics that could include garlic, onion, carrot, celery, parsley, basil, or other herbs (such as rosemary for winter sauces), is sautéed in butter or olive oil, or both. The choice of vegetables and aromatics in the *battuto* is often a reflection of regional preferences. After a *battuto* is sautéed it is called a *soffritto*, and it becomes the foundation upon which the sauce is built. In the second approach, the ingredients are combined *a crudo*, that is, raw, in a cold pot with no butter or oil. The sauce is simmered until the proper consistency is achieved. After cooking, extra-virgin olive oil or butter is added for flavor.

A good tomato sauce can consist of as few as three ingredients—tomatoes, olive oil or butter, and salt—or it can include aromatics as well. More elaborate sauces may begin with a *battuto*, as just described, or may contain one or more meats, *prosciutto crudo*, wine, or cream. Adding carrots, celery, and herbs gives the mixture body and makes for a more fruity sauce.

Essentially, complex sauces are built on the foundations of the simple ones, such as the basic sauces found in chapter one. Each ingredient contributes something different: vegetables add body and flavor; butter or cream imparts sweetness and smoothness; wine deepens the flavor.

Tomato paste, used as a binding agent, is only necessary when using tomatoes packed in juices. Tomatoes packed in purée don't need the thickening feature of the paste. The strong, concentrated nature of tomato paste adds flavor to sauces, but too much imparts a sharp, even bitter taste. (A rule of thumb is to use no more than 3 tablespoons paste to 2½ cups tomatoes.) Sauces can be made exclusively with tomato paste diluted with water, however, if they contain other ingredients whose flavor characteristics create a balance with the sharpness of the tomato concentrate.

Quick Cooked or Long Simmered?

Length of cooking is an important consideration in the success of tomato sauce. Only when tomato sauce includes meat should it undergo extended cooking. Long, gentle simmering is necessary to tenderize meat, and to allow its flavor to marry with other ingredients. But the notion of cooking a non-meat tomato sauce for hours is misdirected. A *sugo di pomodoro* implies a quickly cooked sauce with fresh, fruity flavor. To achieve this, the shorter the cooking time necessary to evaporate excess liquid, the better. Sauces cook by evaporation. It takes at least ten minutes before the acidic flavor of the tomato is transformed and the tomatoes sweeten, then another ten to twenty minutes—depending on the tomato—for excess liquid to evaporate. Thus a quick sauce can be made in twenty to twenty-five minutes. The cooking time for a nonmeat sauce should generally not exceed forty-five minutes.

Strained Versus Unstrained

A technique used by Italians to create a smooth, uniform consistency is to pass tomato sauces through a food mill after cooking. Puréeing the sauce in a blender or food processer is not a substitute for the food mill because only the mill holds the seeds back. In contrast, the blades of a blender or a food processor macerates them, releasing their bitter flavor into the sauce. Italians often strain sauces in this manner, while Americans are somewhat unfamiliar with the procedure. The matter of strained versus unstrained tomato sauce is both a question of preference and of the compatability of the sauce with whatever food it will anoint. In regard to pasta, ribbon or strand types are particularly compatible with strained sauces, while short, stubby macaroni cuts are better suited to the chunky texture of unstrained sauces.

Recipes

CHAPTER ONE

Sughi di pomodoro
Basic Tomato Sauces

Purè di pomodori freschi
LIGHT PURÉED FRESH TOMATO SAUCE

Purè leggero di pomodoro
LIGHT PURÉED TOMATO SAUCE

Salsa di pomodoro semplice alla meridionale
QUICK, SIMPLE SOUTHERN-STYLE TOMATO SAUCE

Salsa di pomodoro rustica
RUSTIC TOMATO SAUCE

Salsa veloce di pomodoro con burro
QUICK-COOKED TOMATO SAUCE WITH BUTTER

Pomarola (Pummarola)
NEAPOLITAN TOMATO SAUCE

*S*ughi di pomodoro are distinguished from *salse di pomodoro* in that they are simple sauces comprised of tomato and only a few supporting ingredients. A *sugo* (pronounced soo'go), singular of *sughi* (pronounced soo'ghee), can stand on its own with pasta or other dishes, or it can also be used as a foundation for other sauces (*salse*). In America, we would define a *sugo* as an "all-purpose" sauce. *Salse di pomodoro,* on the other hand, are tomato sauces flavored with other ingredients, such as wine or vinegar, vegetables, or seafood.

An all-purpose tomato sauce is so basic to Italian cooking that it is often made in large quantities. It is used liberally with cooked vegetables; as a topping for *pizze*; spooned over *polpettone* (meat loaf) and meat, poultry, and seafood dishes; pooled alongside or stirred into *polenta* and rice; and as a sauce for all kinds of pasta. Another use of a *sugo* is in a baked dish (*pasticcio*), either alone or in alternating layers with creamy *béchamel*.

The components of a basic tomato sauce can be as simple as tomatoes and olive oil with a scrap of basil for fragrance. More complex *sughi* are built on *odori*, literally, "scents," by which the Italians mean a combination of vegetables and aromatics that usually include onion, garlic, carrots, celery, and parsley, and possibly sage and rosemary. If basil is included, it is usually added closer to the end of the cooking time. Only fresh ingredients will do—never dried garlic or onion powder, dried parsley flakes, and the like.

Basic sauces never include oregano or green peppers, which are common ingredients in tomato sauces outside of Italy. Such intense flavors are distractions. Nor do they include sugar (although a pinch is sometimes added to foil the acidity of the tomatoes), honey, or other sweeteners. The idea is to make a tomato sauce taste quintessentially like tomato, and to include only those ingredients that support or complement.

Despite their simplicity, there are infinite variations on the theme of basic tomato sauces. The six that are included in this chapter represent various techniques and different styles of sauces: some are fruity while others are pure tomato; some are refined while others are rustic. The success of each depends primarily on the flavor of the tomatoes, the freshness of the supporting ingredients, and in the recipes that call for it, the quality of the olive oil.

Purè di pomodori freschi
LIGHT PURÉED FRESH TOMATO SAUCE

This is one of the most classic, common, and versatile sauces using fresh tomatoes. It can be mated with virtually any pasta cut, fresh or dried, or serve as a foundation for more complex sauces. It is ideal as a sauce for poached eggs (slip the eggs right into the sauce instead of water to cook), or can be combined with cooked vegetables, spooned over grilled or baked meats and seafood or *polpettone* (meat loaf), or used in baked *polenta*, pasta, or bean dishes.

Pellegrino Artusi prescribed a similar method for this classic tomato sauce in his *La scienza in cucina e l'arte di mangiar bene* (the science in cooking and the art of eating well), published in 1891, although his recipe calls for the addition of celery and parsley. They can be added, but I like to keep the sauce perfectly simple when I have excellent tomatoes, so as not to distract from their fresh flavor. I always include carrot, however, which adds natural sweetness and body to the sauce. Butter is swirled in at the last minute for additional complementary sweetness and for good consistency, but extra-virgin olive oil can be used in its place. The velvety character of this sauce can only be obtained through the use of a food mill. Do not attempt to purée it in a food processor or blender, as only a food mill will hold back any errant seeds and create the proper smooth-textured sauce.

2½ POUNDS FRESH, SWEET, MATURE VINE-RIPENED
    PLUM TOMATOES
1 SMALL CARROT, SCRAPED AND GRATED OR CHOPPED
¼ SMALL RED OR YELLOW ONION, FINELY SLICED OR
    CHOPPED
5 FRESH BASIL LEAVES, TORN, PLUS ADDITIONAL BASIL
    LEAVES FOR SERVING
½ TEASPOON SALT
3 TABLESPOONS UNSALTED BUTTER OR EXTRA-
    VIRGIN OLIVE OIL

Cut out the tough area around the core of each tomato. Cut the tomatoes into halves crosswise and squeeze out the seeds, then chop coarsely. Place them in a heavy saucepan with the carrot, onion, the 5 basil leaves, and salt. Bring to a boil, then reduce the heat to medium. Simmer, uncovered, for 20 minutes, stirring frequently to prevent the tomatoes from sticking to the bottom of the pan. At this point, a fairly thick mixture should have formed. If it is excessively watery, simmer for an additional 5 to 10 minutes. Remove from the heat.

When the mixture has cooled somewhat, pass it through a food mill positioned over a clean saucepan, being sure to press the remaining pastelike mixture thoroughly in order to extract as much fiber as possible. You should have a light sauce, thick enough to coat a spoon. If the sauce is too thin, simmer it, uncovered, for another 10 minutes or so to evaporate it further. Just before serving, tear the remaining basil leaves into small pieces and stir them in along with the butter or olive oil. Check for seasoning.

YIELD: Makes approximately 2 cups. This recipe is sufficient for saucing 1 pound of pasta.

AHEAD-OF-TIME NOTE: The sauce can be made 4 to 5 days in advance of using and stored tightly covered in the refrigerator, or it can be frozen for up to 3 months. Whether storing it in the refrigerator or freezer, leave out the remaining basil and butter or olive oil. Stir them into the sauce after reheating.

Purè leggero di pomodoro
LIGHT PURÉED TOMATO SAUCE

Made with canned tomatoes, this versatile sauce is light and smooth and has an unadulterated tomato taste because there is no oil or butter—no *soffritto*—incorporated at the outset. There is also no garlic or onion, so the sauce has a particularly clean, clear tomato flavor. The tomatoes are simmered until enough of the juice evaporates to form a properly thick sauce. The sauce is then strained through a food mill to achieve its velvety smooth texture, and extra-virgin olive oil is added only after cooking is completed. The oil enhances the smoothness of the sauce and, in the absence of heat, imparts its full rich flavor.

Use this sauce as a condiment for chicken, fish, or other seafood, and for various vegetable fritters and rice croquettes. It is a good sauce for *spaghettini*, a light, dried pasta cut, and it is ideal with potato *gnocchi*.

5 CUPS CANNED, PEELED PLUM TOMATOES IN JUICE
¼ CUP EXTRA-VIRGIN OLIVE OIL
½ TEASPOON SALT, OR TO TASTE
FRESHLY MILLED WHITE OR BLACK PEPPER TO TASTE
3 TABLESPOONS CHOPPED FRESH BASIL

Drain the tomatoes, reserving their juice for another use. Using your hands, a fork, or a potato masher, crush or mash the tomatoes and transfer to a saucepan. Place over medium-low heat and simmer uncovered, stirring occasionally, until thickened, about 40 minutes. Remove from the heat.

When the mixture has cooled somewhat, pass it through a food mill positioned over a clean saucepan, being sure to press out as much of the pulp as possible. A smooth, light but substantial sauce will result.

When you are ready to use the sauce, return it to the saucepan and allow it to come just to a simmer. Remove from the heat and stir in the olive oil, salt, pepper, and basil.

YIELD: Makes approximately 2 cups. This recipe is sufficient for saucing 1 pound of pasta.

VARIATION: Add 4 tablespoons unsalted butter in place of the olive oil.

AHEAD-OF-TIME NOTE: The sauce can be made 4 to 5 days in advance of using and stored tightly covered in the refrigerator, or it can be frozen for up to 3 months. Whether storing it in the refrigerator or freezer, leave out the olive oil (or butter), basil, and pepper. Stir them into the sauce after reheating.

Salsa di pomodoro semplice alla meridionale
QUICK, SIMPLE SOUTHERN-STYLE TOMATO SAUCE

While this is one of the quickest tomato sauces you can make, it is delicious in its humble simplicity. Used unsieved, it is very chunky and thick, and thus suitable for ribbon or strand dried pasta cuts or short macaroni cuts such as *pennette* or medium-sized shells. When sieved, it has countless uses as a basic sauce.

4 CUPS CANNED, PEELED PLUM TOMATOES IN JUICE

6 TABLESPOONS EXTRA-VIRGIN OLIVE OIL, PLUS ADDITIONAL EXTRA-VIRGIN OLIVE OIL

4 LARGE CLOVES GARLIC, BRUISED

2/3 TEASPOON SALT, OR TO TASTE

4 LARGE FRESH BASIL OR MINT LEAVES, CHOPPED

Drain the tomatoes, reserving their juice for another use. Using your fingers, push out the excess seeds. Using your hands, a fork, or a potato masher, crush or mash the tomatoes well. Set aside.

In a saucepan over medium-low heat, warm the 6 tablespoons olive oil and garlic together, heating gently until the garlic is golden, 1 or 2 minutes. Add the tomatoes, salt, and basil or mint. Simmer gently for 15 minutes.

If you want a chunkier sauce, remove and discard the garlic cloves, if desired. Remove from the heat and stir in an additional drizzle (1 or 2 tablespoons) of extra-virgin olive oil.

If a very smooth sauce is desired, do not add the additional oil. Allow the sauce to cool somewhat, then position a food mill over a clean saucepan and pass the sauce through it, including the garlic cloves, if desired. Be sure to press out as much of the pulp as possible. Place over medium heat just long enough for the sauce to heat through, about 3 minutes. Remove from the heat and stir in the additional drizzle of extra-virgin olive oil.

If using mint in the sauce, pass freshly grated *pecorino* cheese at the table; if using basil, serve with freshly grated *pecorino* or *parmigiano*.

YIELD: Makes approximately 3 cups. Two cups are sufficient for saucing 1 pound of pasta.

AHEAD-OF-TIME NOTE: The sauce can be made 4 to 5 days in advance of using and stored tightly covered in the refrigerator, or it can be frozen for up to 3 months. Whether storing it in the refrigerator or freezer, leave out the remaining 1 or 2 tablespoons olive oil and the basil or mint. Stir them into the sauce after reheating.

Salsa di pomodoro rustica
RUSTIC TOMATO SAUCE

This is a chunky, pungent sauce, rustic in character due to its unsieved texture and the prominence of garlic. It goes well with both dried pasta and freshly made *gnocchi* or *ravioli*.

2½ CUPS CANNED, PEELED PLUM TOMATOES IN JUICE
3 TABLESPOONS EXTRA-VIRGIN OLIVE OIL
1 LARGE CLOVE GARLIC, FINELY CHOPPED, GRATED, OR
   PASSED THROUGH A GARLIC PRESS
2 TABLESPOONS TOMATO PASTE
2 OR 3 FRESH BASIL LEAVES
¼ TEASPOON SALT, OR TO TASTE
FRESHLY MILLED BLACK PEPPER TO TASTE

Drain the tomatoes, reserving their juice. Strain the captured juice to hold back the seeds. Using your fingers, push out the excess seeds from each tomato. Using your hands, a fork, or a potato masher, crush or mash the tomatoes well. Set the tomatoes and juice aside.

In a cold saucepan over medium-low heat, warm 2 tablespoons of the olive oil and the garlic together, and sauté until the garlic is soft but not colored, 3 to 4 minutes. Add the tomato paste and stir; then add the tomatoes and their juice. Simmer over low heat, uncovered, until enough of the liquid evaporates to form a sauce that will coat a spoon, about 25 minutes.

Tear the basil into small pieces and stir them into the sauce along with the salt. Simmer for another minute or two. Remove from the heat and stir in the pepper and the remaining 1 tablespoon olive oil.

YIELD: Makes approximately 2 cups. This recipe is sufficient for saucing 1 pound of pasta.

VARIATION: Northerners tend to use onion rather than garlic in this sauce. Substitute 1 small red, white, or yellow onion, chopped, for the garlic.

AHEAD-OF-TIME NOTE: The sauce can be made 4 to 5 days in advance of using and stored tightly covered in the refrigerator, or it can be frozen for up to 3 months. Whether storing it in the refrigerator or freezer, leave out the basil, pepper, and remaining 1 tablespoon olive oil. Stir them into the sauce after reheating.

Salsa veloce di pomodoro con burro
QUICK-COOKED TOMATO SAUCE WITH BUTTER

A variation on the preceding quick southern recipe (page 45), this chunky sauce, because it is butter based, is suitable for both delicate fresh pasta, including stuffed pasta, and dried pasta. Flavor it as you like, adding chopped fresh basil or parsley after cooking.

5 CUPS CANNED, PEELED PLUM TOMATOES IN JUICE
1 SMALL RED OR WHITE ONION, MINCED
8 TABLESPOONS UNSALTED BUTTER
2/3 TEASPOON SALT
FRESHLY MILLED WHITE OR BLACK PEPPER TO TASTE
3 TABLESPOONS CHOPPED FRESH BASIL OR ITALIAN
    PARSLEY, OR TO TASTE

Drain the tomatoes, reserving their juice for another use. Using your fingers, push out the excess seeds from each tomato. Chop the tomatoes, or using your hands, a fork, or a potato masher, crush or mash the tomatoes well. Set aside.

In a large saucepan over low heat, combine the onion and 6 tablespoons of the butter. Sauté gently until the onion begins to color but is not browned, about 12 minutes. Add the tomatoes and salt and simmer to blend the flavors, about 15 minutes.

Remove from the heat and stir in the remaining 2 tablespoons butter, the pepper, and basil or parsley just before serving.

YIELD: Makes approximately 3 cups. Two cups are sufficient for saucing 1 pound of pasta.

AHEAD-OF-TIME NOTE: The sauce can be made 4 to 5 days in advance of using and stored tightly covered in the refrigerator, or it can be frozen for up to 3 months. Whether storing it in the refrigerator or freezer, leave out the remaining 2 tablespoons butter, pepper, and basil or parsley. Stir them into the sauce after reheating.

Pomarola (Pummarola)
NEAPOLITAN TOMATO SAUCE

Pomarola, or *pummarola* in the local dialect, is the classic Neapolitan sauce for spaghetti and macaroni, made with fresh tomatoes in season or with canned tomatoes out of season. Because it begins with a generous *battuto* (vegetable base), it is very fruity and fragrant and has a great deal of texture. It is well suited to firmer textures of dried pasta; *linguine* and *bucatini* are especially compatible with it. When sieved, *pomarola* can be used as a foundation for other sauces and *ragù*.

2½ CUPS CANNED, PEELED PLUM TOMATOES IN JUICE,
   OR 2½ POUNDS FRESH, SWEET, MATURE VINE-RIPENED
   PLUM TOMATOES, PEELED, SEEDED, AND CHOPPED
4 TABLESPOONS EXTRA-VIRGIN OLIVE OIL
2 LARGE CLOVES GARLIC, BRUISED
1 SMALL RED ONION, FINELY CHOPPED
1 MEDIUM CELERY STALK, INCLUDING LEAVES, FINELY
   CHOPPED
1 SMALL CARROT, SCRAPED AND FINELY CHOPPED
1 TABLESPOON CHOPPED FRESH ITALIAN PARSLEY
SMALL HANDFUL OF CHOPPED FRESH BASIL
2 TABLESPOONS TOMATO PASTE
SCANT ½ TEASPOON SALT, OR TO TASTE
FRESHLY MILLED BLACK OR WHITE PEPPER TO TASTE

If using canned tomatoes, drain the tomatoes reserving their juice. Strain the captured tomato juice to hold back the seeds. Using your fingers, push out the excess seeds from each tomato. Chop the tomatoes and set the tomatoes and juice aside. If using fresh tomatoes, slip them into a saucepan of rapidly boiling water and blanch for 30 to 45 seconds. Drain the tomatoes and immediately plunge them into cold water. Using a paring knife, lift off the skins and cut out the tough core portions. Cut the tomatoes into quarters lengthwise and, using your fingers, push out the excess seeds. Chop the tomatoes and set aside.

In a saucepan over medium-low heat, warm 3 tablespoons of the olive oil, the garlic, and onion together, and sauté until the garlic is golden and the onion is translucent, 4 to 5 minutes. Then add the celery, carrot, parsley, and basil, and sauté until the vegetables are soft, about 10 minutes.

Press down on the vegetables with the back of a wooden spoon to release their flavors. Add the tomato paste and continue to sauté for 3 minutes. Then add the tomatoes and their juice, cover partially, and simmer gently until thickened, about 45 minutes.

Remove and discard the garlic cloves and season to taste with salt and pepper. If a chunky sauce is desired, remove from the heat and stir in the remaining 1 tablespoon olive oil. If a smooth sauce is desired, allow it to cool somewhat. Position a food mill over a clean saucepan and pass the sauce through it, being sure to press out as much of the pulp as possible. Place over medium heat just long enough for the sauce to heat through, about 3 minutes. Remove from the heat and stir in the remaining 1 tablespoon olive oil.

YIELD: Makes approximately 2 cups. This recipe is sufficient for saucing 1 pound of pasta.

AHEAD-OF-TIME NOTE: The sauce can be made 4 to 5 days in advance of using and stored tightly covered in the refrigerator, or it can be frozen for up to 3 months. Whether storing it in the refrigerator or freezer, leave out the remaining 1 tablespoon olive oil. Stir it into the sauce after reheating.

CHAPTER TWO

Salse di pomodoro sbrigative
Quick Tomato Sauces

Salsa cruda di pomodoro e mozzarella
UNCOOKED TOMATO SAUCE WITH MOZZARELLA

Salsa rossa cruda
UNCOOKED RED SAUCE

Salsa rossa cruda con olive nere
UNCOOKED TOMATO SAUCE WITH BLACK OLIVES

COOKED SAUCES

Salsa di pomodoro piccante con pancetta
TOMATO SAUCE WITH BACON AND HOT PEPPER

Salsa di pomodori freschi
FRESH TOMATO SAUCE

Salsa di pomodoro alla pizzaiola
TOMATO SAUCE WITH GARLIC, PARSLEY, AND OREGANO

Salsa portoghese
"PORTUGUESE" SAUCE WITH WHITE WINE AND LEMON

Salsa rossa con peperoni
RED SAUCE WITH SWEET PEPPERS

I am not a proponent of "fast food" of any description. As I see it, the pleasures of life, eating being one, are worth devoting time to. But today, it is nearly impossible for many people to spend a great deal of time marketing and cooking. In any case, no one could argue that it is more enjoyable to eat great food than to spend endless hours in its preparation. One of the best things about Italian cooking is that its directness makes it inherently simple to prepare. Consequently, much of it *is* "fast food." Certainly, many tomato sauces fit this category.

Some of the recipes in this chapter (and others in this book as well) can be prepared in the length of time it takes to bring a kettle of water to a boil for pasta or to grill a steak or hamburger. None should take longer than half an hour. At the end, the sauces can at once be mixed with the pasta or spooned alongside the steak or hamburger.

Today's marketplace offers many inducements to avoid making sauces at home. Elaborately and beautifully packaged bottles promising to deliver great flavor are to be found everywhere. But no bottled sauce can equal one that is made in your own kitchen. Even the simplest homemade sauce, prepared with fresh or canned tomatoes and properly executed, will deliver a clear, fresh tomato taste that preserved sauces cannot achieve.

Recipes for both cooked and uncooked sauces follow. Throughout this book, recipes for cooked sauces specify the use of plum tomatoes because their thick walls and lower seed content make them the best choice for the saucepan. Plum tomatoes are not specified in recipes for uncooked tomato sauces, however. In preparing raw sauces, it is the flavor of the tomato that counts. In fact, it is especially important for all these quick sauces to be made with only the sweetest, most flavorful tomatoes available, whether fresh or canned, plum variety or not. It is equally critical that all the other ingredients be of the highest quality, for the simplicity of the recipes causes each ingredient to stand out.

Salsa cruda di pomodoro
UNCOOKED TOMATO SAUCE

Because this sauce and its variations are uncooked, it is important to use high-quality extra-virgin olive oil, as its rich flavor will be experienced directly. There is no need to peel the tomatoes, although peeling produces a somewhat smoother sauce. The decision is both a matter of personal taste and of convenience. This sauce can only be as good as the tomatoes used, however. Put simply, this is not a sauce to be made with anything but fresh summer tomatoes that have ripened well on the vine and are flavorful and sweet. The basil, too, should be fresh rather than dried. The variations involve using another herb in place of the basil and adding imported black olives. You can also substitute 3 tablespoons finely chopped red onion for garlic. This sauce is excellent with various dried pasta cuts, including *fusilli*, but it is especially good with spaghetti. There is no need for grated cheese.

2 POUNDS FRESH, SWEET, MATURE VINE-RIPENED
  TOMATOES
1 LARGE CLOVE GARLIC, FINELY MINCED
5 TABLESPOONS EXTRA-VIRGIN OLIVE OIL
1/4 CUP FRESH BASIL LEAVES, TORN INTO SMALL PIECES
1/2 TEASPOON SALT, OR TO TASTE
FRESHLY MILLED BLACK PEPPER TO TASTE

Cut out the tough area around the core of each tomato and cut the tomatoes into quarters lengthwise. Using your fingers, push out the excess seeds. Chop the tomatoes coarsely or cut them into fine dice. Place the tomatoes in the bowl in which you will serve the pasta.

    Add the oil, basil, salt, and pepper to the tomatoes and stir to mix well. Allow the sauce to stand at room temperature while the pasta cooks.

YIELD: Makes approximately 2 cups. This recipe is sufficient for saucing 1 pound of pasta.

VARIATION WITH MARJORAM OR OREGANO: Use 1½ tablespoons fresh marjoram leaves or oregano leaves in place of the basil.

VARIATION WITH OLIVES: Add 1/4 to 1/3 cup Niçoise, Gaeta, or other sharply flavored imported black olives, pitted and sliced. Do not use the bland canned variety.

AHEAD-OF-TIME NOTE: Make the sauce up to 4 hours in advance. Cover and leave at room temperature until ready to serve.

Salsa puttanesca cruda
UNCOOKED HARLOT'S SAUCE

Perhaps because of its somewhat racy title, this sauce became fashionable in America some years ago. There are countless versions of it, of which this is only one. The cooked version (page 75) is perhaps better known. This is the summer version, which, like all uncooked tomato sauces, can only be made with impeccably fresh, sweet, vine-ripened tomatoes. As with other uncooked tomato sauces, the tomatoes may be peeled before cutting and seeding them, but if you prefer, leave the skin on. The amount of olives, capers, and pepper should be adjusted to taste. Recommended pasta cuts for this sauce are medium-sized macaroni such as *pennette* (little quills) or *fusilli*. There is no need for grated cheese.

2 POUNDS FRESH, SWEET, MATURE VINE-RIPENED
 TOMATOES
1/3 CUP EXTRA-VIRGIN OLIVE OIL
2 LARGE CLOVES GARLIC, MINCED
1/4 CUP PITTED AND SLICED, SHARPLY FLAVORED
 IMPORTED BLACK OLIVES SUCH AS GAETA, NIÇOISE,
 OR KALAMATA
1 TABLESPOON DRAINED SMALL CAPERS
1/4 TEASPOON RED PEPPER FLAKES, OR TO TASTE
1/2 TEASPOON SALT, OR TO TASTE
2 TEASPOONS FRESH OREGANO OR MARJORAM LEAVES
1 TABLESPOON CHOPPED FRESH ITALIAN PARSLEY

Cut out the tough area around the core of each tomato and cut the tomatoes into quarters lengthwise. Using your fingers, push out the excess seeds. Chop the tomatoes coarsely or cut them into fine dice. Place the tomatoes in the bowl in which you will serve the pasta.

Add the olive oil, garlic, olives, capers, pepper flakes, salt, oregano or marjoram, and parsley to the tomatoes and stir to mix well. Allow the sauce to stand at room temperature while the pasta cooks.

YIELD: Makes approximately 2 cups. This recipe is sufficient for saucing 1 pound of pasta.

AHEAD-OF-TIME NOTE: Make the sauce up to 4 hours in advance. Cover and leave at room temperature until ready to serve.

Salsa cruda di pomodoro alla Flavia

FLAVIA'S UNCOOKED TOMATO AND AVOCADO SAUCE

The original version of this raw sauce, invented by my Italian friend and excellent cook Flavia Destefanis, appeared in my first book, *Pasta Classica: The Art of Italian Pasta Cooking*. It was a sly addition to the established classics, but I knew it would go over as big as tomatoes did in the encounter between the New World and the Old. My hunch proved correct. Now, in the nearly ten years since *Pasta Classica* first came out, the recipe appears on the box of one of Italy's best factory pastas, and it has become a favorite of professional chefs and home cooks alike because it is so easy and so good. Here is a new twist on the original recipe.

Spaghetti is the best pasta choice. Take care not to overcook it, or to overdrain it. It is essential that the pasta be dripping wet when tossed with the sauce to enable the avocado to merge with some of the pasta cooking water, thus "saucing" the strands. The sauce is also an excellent condiment for spooning over swordfish or other firm, dry-fleshed grilled or roasted white fish.

1½ POUNDS FRESH, SWEET, MATURE VINE-RIPENED TOMATOES OR SWEET, RIPE CHERRY TOMATOES

4 LARGE FRESH BASIL LEAVES, TORN INTO VERY SMALL PIECES OR CHOPPED

1 LARGE CLOVE GARLIC, FINELY CHOPPED OR PASSED THROUGH A GARLIC PRESS

5 TABLESPOONS EXTRA-VIRGIN OLIVE OIL

GENEROUS ½ TEASPOON SALT, OR TO TASTE

FRESHLY MILLED BLACK OR WHITE PEPPER TO TASTE

1 LARGE, RIPE (BUT NOT SPOTTED) HASS AVOCADO

Cut out the tough area around the core of each tomato and cut the tomatoes into quarters lengthwise. Using your fingers, push out excess seeds. Cut the tomatoes into rough dice. Place the tomatoes in the bowl in which you will serve the pasta, or in a sauce dish if using with fish. Add the basil, garlic, olive oil, salt, and pepper.

Insert a knife into the avocado at the top, where the navel is. Cut into the avocado until you reach the seed, then make a clean incision all the way around the length of the fruit. Twist the halves in opposite directions to open the avocado. The seed should fall right out. Peel and thinly slice each half crosswise; then cut the slices further into small strips or dice. Add the avocado to the bowl with the other ingredients. Toss to mix and allow to stand at room temperature while the pasta or fish cooks.

YIELD: Makes approximately 2½ cups. This recipe is sufficient for saucing 1 pound of pasta.

AHEAD-OF-TIME NOTE: Make the sauce up to 2 hours in advance. Cover and leave at room temperature until ready to serve.

Salsa cruda di pomodoro e rucola
UNCOOKED TOMATO SAUCE WITH ROCKET

This surprising sauce, which calls for peppery rocket (arugula) leaves, makes a delicious topping for fried breaded veal or chicken breast or for grilled meats. It is also a natural with spaghetti.

1 SMALL BUNCH ROCKET (TO YIELD 1 CUP PACKED
   LEAVES)
¼ CUP EXTRA-VIRGIN OLIVE OIL
2½ TABLESPOONS CHOPPED RED ONION
¼ TEASPOON SALT, OR TO TASTE
FRESHLY MILLED BLACK PEPPER TO TASTE
1 POUND FRESH, SWEET, MATURE VINE-RIPENED
   TOMATOES

Wash the rocket under cold running water, then place it in a bowl. Add cold water to cover and allow it to soak while preparing the remaining ingredients.

Combine the olive oil, onion, salt, and pepper in the bowl in which you will serve the pasta, or in a sauce dish if using with meats. Cut out the tough area around the core of each tomato and cut the tomatoes into quarters lengthwise. Using your fingers, push out the excess seeds. Chop the tomatoes coarsely and add them to the bowl with the oil mixture.

Drain the rocket and then rinse in several changes of cold water to be sure there is no trace of sand. Remove any yellow leaves and tough stems. Dry the rocket thoroughly with clean kitchen towels or in a salad spinner. Chop it coarsely and add it to the bowl with the other ingredients. Toss to mix well. Allow the sauce to stand at room temperature for 30 minutes before using.

YIELD: Makes approximately 2 cups. This recipe is sufficient for saucing 1 pound of pasta.

VARIATION: Substitute 1 large clove garlic, minced, for the red onion.

AHEAD-OF-TIME NOTE: Make the sauce up to 4 hours in advance. Cover and leave at room temperature until ready to serve.

Salsa cruda di pomodoro e mozzarella
UNCOOKED TOMATO SAUCE WITH MOZZARELLA

Another uncooked sauce perfect for pasta. But again, it is only as good as the ingredients that go into it. In addition to using sweet, vine-ripened tomatoes, it is essential to use tender, milky fresh mozzarella, not the shrink-wrapped commercial variety that is sold in supermarkets. Fresh mozzarella, made daily, is commonly sold in Italian specialty-food shops (avoid the tasteless, saltless variety). Medium-sized concave macaroni such as shells or *gnocchi* are ideal pasta cuts for this sauce, as they will cradle the cheese and other ingredients.

1½ POUNDS FRESH, SWEET, MATURE VINE-RIPENED
    TOMATOES
½ CUP EXTRA-VIRGIN OLIVE OIL
¼ CUP FRESH BASIL LEAVES, TORN INTO SMALL PIECES
    OR CHOPPED, OR ¼ CUP CHOPPED FRESH ITALIAN
    PARSLEY
½ POUND FRESH MOZZARELLA, CUT INTO SMALL DICE
2 TABLESPOONS DRAINED SMALL CAPERS
¼ TEASPOON RED PEPPER FLAKES, OR TO TASTE
1 TEASPOON SALT, OR TO TASTE

Cut out the tough area around the core of each tomato and cut the tomatoes into quarters lengthwise. Using your fingers, push out the excess seeds. Cut the tomatoes into rough dice or chop them coarsely. Place the tomatoes in the bowl in which you will serve the pasta. Add the olive oil, basil or parsley, mozzarella, capers, red pepper flakes, and salt to the tomatoes and stir to mix well. Allow the sauce to stand at room temperature while the pasta cooks.

YIELD: Makes approximately 2 cups. This recipe is sufficient for saucing 1 pound of pasta.

AHEAD-OF-TIME NOTE: Make the sauce up to 4 hours in advance. Cover and leave at room temperature until ready to serve.

Salsa rossa cruda
UNCOOKED RED SAUCE

This oniony cold tomato sauce is a traditional Tuscan accompaniment for boiled beef or chicken, but it can also serve as a condiment for grilled meats and fish and for egg dishes. A small quantity of bread crumbs (about 1 teaspoon in this recipe) is sometimes added to thicken the sauce, but I don't find it necessary. Serve at room temperature.

1¼ POUNDS FRESH, SWEET, MATURE VINE-RIPENED
    TOMATOES, OR 1¼ CUPS CANNED, PEELED PLUM
    TOMATOES IN JUICE
1 SMALL CLOVE GARLIC, MINCED
1 SMALL RED ONION, CHOPPED
6 TABLESPOONS EXTRA-VIRGIN OLIVE OIL
½ TEASPOON SWEET PAPRIKA
PINCH OF RED PEPPER FLAKES, OR TO TASTE
½ TEASPOON SALT, OR TO TASTE
2 TABLESPOONS RED WINE VINEGAR
2 TEASPOONS CHOPPED FRESH ITALIAN PARSLEY
    (OPTIONAL)

If using fresh tomatoes, cut out the tough area around the core of each tomato and cut the tomatoes into quarters lengthwise. Using your fingers, push out the excess seeds. Chop the tomatoes coarsely and place in a colander for 5 minutes to drain off the excess juice. If using canned tomatoes, drain the tomatoes, reserving their juice for another use. Using your fingers, push out the excess seeds from each tomato. Coarsely chop the tomatoes.

Combine all the ingredients, except the parsley (if using), in a blender or food processor. Grind together, taking care not to overprocess the mixture to a purée. Stir in the parsley.

YIELD: Makes approximately 1¼ cups.

AHEAD-OF-TIME NOTE: This sauce can be made up to 1 week in advance, covered tightly, and refrigerated. Leave out the parsley until ready to use. Bring the sauce to room temperature before serving, and stir in the parsley.

Salsa rossa cruda con olive nere
UNCOOKED TOMATO SAUCE WITH BLACK OLIVES

There are cooked and uncooked versions of *salsa rossa*, a popular red sauce served as a relish with meats, poultry, or fish. In this uncooked version, the use of olives is particularly successful with poached fish dishes, but they may be omitted when serving the sauce with meats. Use only tasty vine-ripened tomatoes, found most easily during the summer when farm stands sell fresh produce.

1½ POUNDS FRESH, SWEET, MATURE VINE-RIPENED
   TOMATOES
1 SMALL CLOVE GARLIC, FINELY CHOPPED OR PASSED
   THROUGH A GARLIC PRESS
⅓ CUP PITTED AND SLICED, SHARPLY FLAVORED
   IMPORTED BLACK OLIVES SUCH AS GAETA, NIÇOISE,
   OR KALAMATA
¼ CUP TORN OR CHOPPED FRESH BASIL
¼ CUP EXTRA-VIRGIN OLIVE OIL
½ TEASPOON SALT, OR TO TASTE
FRESHLY MILLED BLACK PEPPER TO TASTE

Bring a large saucepan three-fourths full of water to a rapid boil. Slip in the tomatoes and blanch for 30 to 45 seconds. Drain the tomatoes and immediately plunge them into cold water. Using a paring knife, lift off the skins and cut out the tough core portions. Cut the tomatoes into quarters lengthwise and, using your fingers, push out the excess seeds. Chop the tomatoes coarsely and place in a colander for 5 minutes to drain off the excess juice.

Transfer the tomatoes to a bowl and add the garlic, olives, basil, olive oil, salt, and pepper. Stir to mix well. Let stand at room temperature for 1 to 3 hours before using.

YIELD: Makes approximately 1¾ cups.

AHEAD-OF-TIME NOTE: This sauce can be made up to 1 day in advance. Cover tightly and refrigerate.

Salsa di pomodoro piccante con pancetta
TOMATO SAUCE WITH BACON AND HOT PEPPER

When this sauce is combined with pasta, most typically *penne*, the dish becomes *penne all'arrabbiata*, literally, "angry" *penne*, owing to the fire given the sauce by the red pepper. The dish is always served with freshly grated *pecorino* cheese, whose salty tanginess is suited to the zesty character of the sauce.

2½ CUPS CANNED, PEELED PLUM TOMATOES IN JUICE
2 OUNCES PANCETTA, SLICED, OR LEAN BACON STRIPS
2 TABLESPOONS EXTRA-VIRGIN OLIVE OIL
1 CLOVE GARLIC, MINCED
¼ TEASPOON RED PEPPER FLAKES
½ TEASPOON SALT

Drain the tomatoes, reserving their juice. Strain the captured juice to hold back the seeds. Using your fingers, push out the excess seeds from each tomato. Roughly chop the tomatoes and set aside with their juice. If using pancetta, cut it into thin strips. If using bacon, drop it into boiling water to cover and blanch for 30 seconds. Drain, rinse in cold water, and drain again. Cut it into thin strips.

Combine the olive oil and the garlic in a cold saucepan. Place the pan over medium-low heat and sauté until the garlic begins to color, 3 or 4 minutes.

Add the pancetta or bacon and continue to sauté over medium-low heat until it colors nicely, about 6 minutes. Add the red pepper flakes, the tomatoes and their juice, and the salt. Simmer uncovered over medium-low heat, stirring occasionally, until the sauce thickens. The sauce should be done in about 20 minutes.

YIELD: Makes approximately 2½ cups. Two cups are sufficient for saucing 1 pound of pasta.

AHEAD-OF-TIME NOTE: The sauce can be made 4 to 5 days in advance of using and stored tightly covered in the refrigerator, or it can be frozen for up to 3 months.

Salsa di pomodori freschi
FRESH TOMATO SAUCE

To me, this fresh, light sauce, aromatic from the abundance of basil used, is one of the most appealing of all tomato sauces, assuming the use of high-quality, impeccably fresh summer tomatoes. Pasta cuts recommended are string or ribbon variety dried pasta such as *spaghettini*, spaghetti, or dried egg *tagliatelle*. The sauce can also be used as the liquid for poaching eggs or it can be spooned alongside a simple frittata or other egg dish.

2½ POUNDS FRESH, SWEET, MATURE VINE-RIPENED
   PLUM TOMATOES
⅓ CUP EXTRA-VIRGIN OLIVE OIL
6 CLOVES GARLIC, BRUISED
½ TEASPOON SEA SALT
GENEROUS HANDFUL OF FRESH BASIL LEAVES, CHOPPED
FRESHLY MILLED WHITE OR BLACK PEPPER TO TASTE

Bring a large saucepan three-fourths full of water to a rapid boil. Slip in the tomatoes and blanch for 30 to 45 seconds. Drain the tomatoes and immediately plunge them into cold water. Using a paring knife, lift off the skins and cut out the tough core portions. Cut the tomatoes into quarters lengthwise and, using your fingers, push out the excess seeds. Chop the tomatoes coarsely and place in a colander to drain for 5 minutes. Set aside.

Meanwhile, in a saucepan, warm the olive oil and garlic together, pressing on the bruised garlic with the back of a wooden spoon to release its juices. When the garlic acquires a rich golden color but has not yet turned brown, after 1 or 2 minutes, remove it and immediately add the tomatoes and salt. Using a fork or, better, a potato masher, press down on the tomatoes to break them up until they are chopped into fairly fine pieces. Increase the heat to high and bring the tomatoes to a simmer. Reduce the heat to medium-low and continue to simmer, stirring occasionally, until the tomatoes acquire a thick, saucelike consistency, stirring occasionally, about 20 minutes.

Remove from the heat and stir in the basil and pepper. Check for seasoning before serving.

YIELD: Makes approximately 2½ cups. Two cups is sufficient for saucing 1 pound of pasta.

AHEAD-OF-TIME NOTE: This sauce can be made up to 1 day in advance of using and stored tightly covered in the refrigerator, or it can be frozen for up to 3 months. Whether storing it in the refrigerator or freezer, leave out the basil and pepper. Stir them into the sauce after reheating.

Salsa di pomodoro alla pizzaiola
TOMATO SAUCE WITH GARLIC, PARSLEY, AND OREGANO

Pizzaiola is a classic sauce of Naples. It is used most characteristically as a condiment for *bistecca*, by which is meant either beef or veal steak, and is slathered, rather than dabbed on. While the sauce is typically made with fresh tomatoes, good canned tomatoes will produce a successful sauce. This lovely, garlicky, herb-bolstered blend is equally happy with roasted or grilled veal or chicken, or with fish, whether it is fried, steamed, grilled, or broiled.

2½ CUPS CANNED, PEELED PLUM TOMATOES IN JUICE,
    OR 2½ POUNDS FRESH, SWEET, MATURE VINE-RIPENED
    PLUM TOMATOES
¼ CUP PLUS 1 TABLESPOON EXTRA-VIRGIN OLIVE OIL
4 MEDIUM CLOVES GARLIC, MINCED
2 TEASPOONS CHOPPED FRESH OREGANO, OR 1
    TEASPOON DRIED OREGANO
2 TABLESPOONS CHOPPED FRESH ITALIAN PARSLEY
½ TEASPOON SALT
FRESHLY MILLED BLACK PEPPER TO TASTE

If using canned tomatoes, drain them, reserving their juice. Strain the captured juice to hold back the seeds. Measure out ¼ cup of the juice and reserve the remaining juice for another use. Using your fingers, push out the excess seeds from each tomato. Coarsely chop the tomatoes and set tomatoes and juice aside. If using fresh tomatoes, slip them into a saucepan of rapidly boiling water and blanch for 30 to 45 seconds. Drain the tomatoes and immediately plunge them into cold water. Drain again and, using a paring knife, lift off the skins and cut out the tough core portions. Cut the tomatoes into quarters lengthwise and, using your fingers, push out the excess seeds. Coarsely chop the tomatoes, transfer them to a bowl, and set aside.

Combine the ¼ cup oil with the garlic in a cold saucepan. Place the pan over medium-low heat and warm the oil, stirring to flavor it well with the minced garlic. Sauté until the garlic softens, 3 to 4 minutes; do not allow it to color. Add the tomatoes and the ¼ cup juice. If using fresh tomatoes, they will give off enough of their own natural juices. Raise the heat to high and cook, stirring occasionally, until a thick consistency is formed, 10 to 12 minutes. Add the oregano, parsley, salt, and pepper and mix well. Remove from the heat and stir in the remaining 1 tablespoon olive oil.

YIELD: Makes approximately 1½ cups.

AHEAD-OF-TIME NOTE: The sauce can be made 3 to 4 days in advance of using and stored tightly covered in the refrigerator, or it can be frozen for up to 3 months. Whether storing it in the refrigerator or freezer, leave out the pepper and the remaining 1 tablespoon olive oil; stir them in before using.

Salsa portoghese
"PORTUGUESE" SAUCE WITH WHITE WINE AND LEMON

The origins of this sauce are unknown, but *portoghese* no doubt refers to its compatibility with seafood, of which the Portuguese are inordinately fond. The presence of lemon makes it a logical condiment for all kinds of fish and shellfish, but the sauce belongs to the genre of red sauces that accompany the boiled meats and poultry so popular in Italian cooking. It is a fine condiment for grilled, baked, or roasted meats, poultry, and fish as well. While part of the fruity olive oil is used in cooking the sauce, much of it is added afterward, so that the full flavors of the oil, unaltered by heat, are experienced.

1¼ CUPS CANNED, PEELED PLUM TOMATOES IN JUICE,
   OR 1¼ POUNDS FRESH, SWEET, MATURE VINE-RIPENED
   TOMATOES
5 TABLESPOONS EXTRA-VIRGIN OLIVE OIL
1 MEDIUM-SIZED RED OR WHITE ONION, QUARTERED
   AND THEN FINELY SLICED
¾ CUP GOOD-QUALITY DRY WHITE WINE
¼ TEASPOON SALT
1 TEASPOON FRESHLY SQUEEZED LEMON JUICE
2 TEASPOONS CHOPPED FRESH ITALIAN PARSLEY
FRESHLY MILLED BLACK OR WHITE PEPPER TO TASTE

If using canned tomatoes, drain them, reserving their juice for another use. Using your fingers, push out the excess seeds from each tomato. Chop the tomatoes and set aside. If using fresh tomatoes, slip them into a saucepan of rapidly boiling water and blanch for 30 to 45 seconds. Drain the tomatoes and immediately plunge them into cold water. Drain again and, using a paring knife, lift off the skins and cut out the tough core portions. Cut the tomatoes into quarters lengthwise and, using your fingers, push out the excess seeds. Chop the tomatoes and place in a colander to drain for 5 minutes. Set aside.

In a saucepan over low heat, warm 3 tablespoons of the oil. Add the onion and sauté gently until very soft, about 10 minutes. Add the wine and simmer gently, uncovered, until the wine evaporates completely, about 10 minutes. Add the tomatoes and salt and continue to cook gently over low heat, stirring occasionally, until a thick consistency is reached, about 15 minutes. Remove from the heat and stir in the remaining 2 tablespoons olive oil, the lemon juice, parsley, and pepper just before serving.

YIELD: Makes approximately 1½ cups.

VARIATION: For a more refined sauce, transfer to a blender before adding the remaining olive oil, lemon juice, parsley, and pepper. Blend for several seconds to purée. Stir in the remaining ingredients and serve.

AHEAD-OF-TIME NOTE: The sauce can be made 4 to 5 days in advance of using and stored tightly covered in the refrigerator, or it can be frozen for up to 3 months. Whether storing it in the refrigerator or freezer, leave out the remaining 2 tablespoons olive oil, the lemon juice, parsley, and pepper. Stir them into the sauce after reheating.

Salsa rossa con peperoni
RED SAUCE WITH SWEET PEPPERS

Another variation—this one cooked—on the classic red sauce served with the famed boiled dinner of Emilia and Tuscany. I find it particularly suitable as a condiment for any type of grilled or roasted beef or veal, and excellent with hamburgers.

1½ POUNDS FRESH, SWEET, MATURE VINE-RIPENED TOMATOES, OR 1½ CUPS CANNED, PEELED PLUM TOMATOES IN JUICE
2 MEDIUM BELL PEPPERS, 1 RED AND 1 YELLOW
4 TABLESPOONS EXTRA-VIRGIN OLIVE OIL
1 SMALL YELLOW ONION, FINELY CHOPPED
2 CLOVES GARLIC, MINCED
1 TABLESPOON DRAINED SMALL CAPERS

If using fresh tomatoes, slip them into a saucepan of rapidly boiling water and blanch for 30 to 45 seconds. Drain the tomatoes and immediately plunge them into cold water. Drain again and, using a paring knife, lift off the skins and cut out the tough core portion. Cut them into quarters lengthwise and, using your fingers, push out the excess seeds. Chop the tomatoes and place in a colander to drain for 5 minutes. If using canned tomatoes, drain them, reserving their juice for another use. Using your fingers, push out the excess seeds from each tomato, then chop the tomatoes and set aside.

Cut the bell peppers in half lengthwise, de-rib them, and remove their stems and seeds. Cut the halves into ½-inch-wide strips, then cut the strips into small dice. Set aside.

In a skillet over low heat, warm 3 tablespoons of the olive oil. Add the onion and garlic and sauté gently, stirring frequently, until they are softened and translucent, 4 or 5 minutes. Add the diced peppers and sauté gently, stirring frequently, for 10 minutes. Add the tomatoes, cover, and cook gently, stirring occasionally, until the peppers are tender, 5 to 8 minutes.

Remove from the heat and stir in the capers and the remaining 1 tablespoon of olive oil. Serve hot, warm, or at room temperature.

YIELD: Makes approximately 2¼ cups.

AHEAD-OF-TIME NOTE: The flavor of this sauce is improved if it is made in advance and allowed to cool; leave out the remaining 1 tablespoon olive oil and the capers until just ready to serve. The sauce can be made 2 or even 3 days in advance of using and stored tightly covered in the refrigerator, or it can be frozen for up to 3 months. Whether storing it in the refrigerator or freezer, leave out the remaining 1 tablespoon olive oil and the capers; stir them in just before using.

CHAPTER THREE

Salse di pomodoro di magro
Hearty Vegetarian Tomato Sauces

Salsa di pomodoro e melanzane
TOMATO SAUCE WITH EGGPLANT

Salsa di pomodoro alla puttanesca, variante calda
TOMATO SAUCE, HARLOT STYLE, HOT VERSION

Salsa di pomodoro con melanzane, peperoni, olive, e capperi
TOMATO SAUCE WITH EGGPLANT, SWEET PEPPER, OLIVES, AND CAPERS

Salsa di pomodoro con funghi freschi e secchi
TOMATO SAUCE WITH FRESH AND DRIED MUSHROOMS

Salsa passata di pomodoro al vino rosso
SIEVED TOMATO SAUCE WITH RED WINE

Salsa di pomodoro e olive nere
TOMATO SAUCE WITH GARLIC AND BLACK OLIVES

Salsa di pomodoro con cipolla e rosmarino
TOMATO SAUCE WITH ONION AND ROSEMARY

Pesto di pomodoro
SUN-DRIED TOMATO PESTO

*I*t wasn't until the twentieth century that meat was commonly eaten in Italy. Between the restrictions of the Catholic church, which forbade meat eating during what amounted to one-third of the calendar year, and the general poverty of the majority of the population until after World War II, few people ate meat in any form. The result was the evolution of a cuisine that is rich in meatless dishes—and meatless sauces.

There are many meatless tomato sauces that rely on vegetables and such standbys of the Italian pantry as olives and capers for variations in flavor. Although wine is more usual in meat sauces, it is sometimes added to vegetarian sauces where it is compatible, to deepen the flavors.

Southern-style sauces are particularly apt to include vegetables, which are in accord with the hot, arid climate. Thus Sicily pairs eggplant with tomatoes as a topping for macaroni, Naples produces a sauce spiked with olives, capers, garlic, and hot pepper, and *salse di pomodoro con funghi* appear throughout the central and southern provinces.

Meatless sauces that fit other broad categories more appropriately appear elsewhere in this book, and can be located in the index.

Salsa di pomodoro e melanzane
TOMATO SAUCE WITH EGGPLANT

When this irresistible sauce is served with pasta, it is called *pasta alla Norma*. The classic way to make it is to fry the cubed eggplant, then add it to the tomato sauce. I also offer a method for making the sauce with roasted eggplant, thus reducing the amount of oil in the recipe (see variation). Recommended pasta cuts for this sauce include *penne, rigatoni, spaghetti, vermicelli, linguine*, and *bucatini*.

1 LARGE EGGPLANT (ABOUT 1¼ POUNDS)
SALT
1 RECIPE QUICK, SIMPLE SOUTHERN-STYLE TOMATO
 SAUCE (PAGE 45), OMITTING THE ADDITIONAL 1
 TABLESPOON OLIVE OIL ADDED AFTER COOKING
OLIVE OIL FOR FRYING

Slice off the stem and navel from the eggplant. Cut the eggplant into 1-inch cubes, place them in a colander, and sprinkle generously with salt. Set the eggplant aside for 40 minutes to allow the bitterness to drain from the seeds.

Meanwhile, make the tomato sauce as directed. When it is done, remove it from the heat and set aside.

Rinse the salt off the eggplant and, using 2 or 3 clean kitchen towels, dry it well. In a large skillet, pour in olive oil to a depth of ½ inch. Place it over medium-high to high heat until the oil is hot enough for the eggplant to sizzle when a cube is added. Add the eggplant in batches, giving the cubes plenty of room to fry properly. When they are golden on all sides, after 5 to 6 minutes in all, use a slotted spoon to lift the eggplant out and transfer it to a platter lined with paper towels to drain.

When all of the eggplant cubes are fried, add them to the tomato sauce and place over medium-low heat. Stir to mix the eggplant and the sauce and heat through. Check for seasoning just before using.

YIELD: Makes approximately 4 cups. This recipe is sufficient for saucing 2 pounds of pasta.

VARIATION: To make this sauce with roasted egg-plant, trim, cut, salt, drain, and dry the eggplant as directed. Meanwhile, preheat an oven to 400 degrees F. In a large bowl, toss the eggplant cubes with 3 tablespoons olive oil. Spread the eggplant in a single layer on baking sheets and bake until golden, about 25 minutes. Add the eggplant to the prepared sauce as above.

AHEAD-OF-TIME NOTE: Because the eggplant loses a certain clarity of flavor when cooked ahead, the sauce is best made on the same day it is to be used. The Quick, Simple Southern-Style Tomato Sauce, however, can be made 4 to 5 days in advance of using and stored tightly covered in the refrigerator, or it can be frozen for up to 3 months. Fry or roast the eggplant shortly before you are ready to cook the sauce and proceed with the recipe.

Salsa di pomodoro alla puttanesca, variante calda
TOMATO SAUCE, HARLOT STYLE, HOT VERSION

There are many, many versions of this zesty southern Italian sauce, named after the harlots of Naples (for the cold version, see page 56). This one is meant to be served with spaghetti. It is important to use tomatoes in their own juices here, not tomatoes in purée or any tomato paste. The reason for this is that all of the other ingredients—garlic, olives, capers, herbs—should stand out as separate elements in the sauce rather than blend together; the purée or paste would bind the ingredients too much. For the same reason, the garlic should be cut into small pieces, not chopped or passed through a garlic press.

2½ CUPS CANNED, PEELED PLUM TOMATOES IN JUICE

3 TABLESPOONS EXTRA-VIRGIN OLIVE OIL

3 LARGE CLOVES GARLIC, CUT INTO SMALL PIECES

3 TABLESPOONS CHOPPED FRESH ITALIAN PARSLEY

1 TEASPOON CHOPPED FRESH OREGANO, OR ½ TEASPOON CRUMBLED DRIED OREGANO

3 ANCHOVY FILLETS PACKED IN OLIVE OIL, DRAINED AND CUT UP

¼ CUP SHARPLY FLAVORED IMPORTED BLACK OLIVES SUCH AS GAETA, NIÇOISE, OR KALAMATA, PITTED AND SLICED

½ TEASPOON RED PEPPER FLAKES

2 TABLESPOONS DRAINED SMALL CAPERS

SALT TO TASTE

Drain the tomatoes, reserving their juice. Strain the captured juices to hold back the seeds. Using your fingers, push out the excess seeds from each tomato. Chop the tomatoes and set tomatoes and juice aside.

In a large skillet, combine the olive oil, garlic, parsley, and oregano. Place over medium-low heat and sauté gently until the garlic softens, 3 to 4 minutes. Do not allow the garlic to brown. Add the anchovies and stir. Then add the tomatoes and juice, the olives, red pepper flakes, and capers. Simmer, stirring frequently, until the sauce thickens, about 20 minutes. Add salt if needed; the saltiness of the anchovies and capers might be enough to your taste.

YIELD: Makes approximately 2½ cups. Two cups are sufficient for saucing 1 pound of pasta.

AHEAD-OF-TIME NOTE: This sauce can be made 3 or 4 days in advance of using and stored tightly covered in the refrigerator, or it can be frozen for up to 3 months.

Salsa di pomodoro con melanzane, peperoni, olive, e capperi
TOMATO SAUCE WITH EGGPLANT, SWEET PEPPER, OLIVES, AND CAPERS

This lively sauce is reminiscent of *caponata*, the Sicilian compote often served as an *antipasto* on the Italian table. It is savory rather than sweet and sour, however. Use it to sauce a short cut of pasta such as *penne*, or as an accompaniment to roasted chicken or fish.

1 MEDIUM EGGPLANT (ABOUT 1 POUND)
½ TEASPOON SALT, PLUS SALT FOR EGGPLANT
2½ CUPS CANNED, PEELED PLUM TOMATOES IN JUICE
1 RED OR YELLOW BELL PEPPER
3 TABLESPOONS EXTRA-VIRGIN OLIVE OIL
3 LARGE CLOVES GARLIC, CHOPPED
8 SHARPLY FLAVORED IMPORTED BLACK OLIVES, SUCH AS GAETA, NIÇOISE, OR KALAMATA, PITTED AND SLICED
2 TEASPOONS DRAINED SMALL CAPERS
2 TABLESPOONS CHOPPED FRESH ITALIAN PARSLEY
2 TABLESPOONS CHOPPED FRESH BASIL
FRESHLY MILLED BLACK OR WHITE PEPPER TO TASTE

Slice off the stem and navel from the eggplant. Cut the eggplant into 1-inch cubes, place them in a colander, and sprinkle generously with salt. Set the eggplant aside for 40 minutes to allow the bitterness to drain from the seeds.

Meanwhile, drain the tomatoes, reserving their juice. Strain the captured tomato juice to hold back the seeds. Measure out ½ cup juice and reserve the remaining juice for another use. Using your fingers, push out the excess seeds from each tomato. Chop the tomatoes and set the tomatoes and juice aside.

Cut the bell pepper in half lengthwise, de-rib the halves, and remove the stem and seeds. Cut the halves into ½-inch-wide strips, and then cut the strips into small dice. Set aside.

Rinse the salt off the eggplant and, using 2 or 3 clean kitchen towels, dry it well. In a saucepan over high heat, combine the olive oil, garlic, eggplant, and bell pepper. Sauté, stirring occasionally, until the eggplant is tender, about 9 minutes. Add the tomatoes and ½ cup juice and the ½ teaspoon salt, reduce the heat to medium, and stir and cook until the mixture is thickened, an additional 10 minutes. Remove from the heat and stir in the olives, capers, parsley, basil, and pepper.

YIELD: Makes approximately 4 cups. Two cups are sufficient for saucing 1 pound pasta.

AHEAD-OF-TIME NOTE: The sauce can be made 3 to 4 days in advance of using and stored tightly covered in the refrigerator, or it can be frozen for up to 3 months. Whether storing it in the refrigerator or freezer, leave out the olives, capers, parsley, basil, and pepper. Stir them into the sauce after reheating.

Salsa di pomodoro con funghi freschi e secchi
TOMATO SAUCE WITH FRESH AND DRIED MUSHROOMS

The bosky flavor of the *porcini* mushrooms and the essence of red wine makes this a rich, full-bodied sauce, delightful with *polenta* as well as pasta. Recommended pasta cuts include spaghetti, *linguine, tagliatelle,* and any short-cut macaroni such as *penne* or *fusilli.*

1 OUNCE DRIED PORCINI MUSHROOMS

1 CUP HOT TAP WATER

2½ CUPS CANNED, PEELED PLUM TOMATOES IN PURÉE

½ POUND CULTIVATED WHITE MUSHROOMS

½ POUND FRESH MUSHROOMS SUCH AS SHIITAKE, OYSTER, CREMINI, PORTOBELLO, OR CHANTERELLE, OR A MIXTURE

3 TABLESPOONS EXTRA-VIRGIN OLIVE OIL

3 LARGE CLOVES GARLIC, CHOPPED

1 LARGE YELLOW ONION, CHOPPED

1 MEDIUM CARROT, SCRAPED AND CHOPPED

2 TEASPOONS CHOPPED FRESH MARJORAM, OR 1 TEA-SPOON CRUMBLED DRIED MARJORAM

3 TABLESPOONS TOMATO PASTE

⅓ CUP GOOD-QUALITY DRY RED WINE

1½ TEASPOONS SALT

Soak and rinse the dried *porcini* as directed on page 101. Squeeze out the excess water and cut them into pieces about the size of your thumbnail. Set aside. Strain the mushroom liquid through a cheese-cloth-lined sieve (or use a paper towel) and reserve.

Meanwhile, drain the tomatoes, reserving the purée. Strain the captured purée to hold back the seeds. Using your fingers, push out the excess seeds from each tomato. Chop the tomatoes and set aside with their purée.

Clean any dirt off all the fresh mushrooms with a soft brush or cloth. Do not wash them. Separate the stems from the caps, discarding the stems if they are tough. Slice the mushroom caps and tender stems thinly.

In a skillet, heat the olive oil and add the garlic, onion, and carrot. Sauté over medium-low heat until the vegetables soften, 10 to 12 minutes. Add the marjoram and *porcini* and sauté gently for 4 to 5 minutes. Add all the fresh mushrooms and sauté gently until softened, 7 to 8 minutes longer.

Add the tomato paste and the reserved mushroom water and stir to combine. Simmer over medium-low heat for 3 to 4 minutes, then add the wine. Cook until the alcohol evaporates, about 3 minutes. Add the tomatoes and purée and the salt. Allow the sauce to simmer until all the mushroom water has evaporated and the sauce has a thick consistency, about 30 minutes. Check for salt and remove from the heat.

YIELD: Makes approximately 2½ cups. Two cups are sufficient for saucing 1 pound of pasta.

AHEAD-OF-TIME NOTE: This sauce can be made 3 or 4 days in advance of using and stored tightly covered in the refrigerator, or it can be frozen for up to 3 months.

Salsa passata di pomodoro al vino rosso
SIEVED TOMATO SAUCE WITH RED WINE

Red wine adds complexity and depth to this sauce; the use of butter makes it silky and sweet. The sauce is suitable for fresh or dried pasta, but it is particularly recommended for homemade egg pasta such as *tagliatelle* and stuffed pasta such as *agnolotti*, *ravioli*, and *manicotti*. If you do not have a food mill, the sauce can be puréed in a food processor, although the result will be less refined.

2½ CUPS CANNED, PEELED PLUM TOMATOES IN JUICE
6 TABLESPOONS UNSALTED BUTTER
1 SMALL WHITE OR RED ONION, MINCED
1 MEDIUM CELERY STALK, MINCED
1 MEDIUM CARROT, SCRAPED AND MINCED
3 TABLESPOONS CHOPPED FRESH BASIL
3 TABLESPOONS TOMATO PASTE
¼ CUP GOOD-QUALITY DRY RED WINE
SALT TO TASTE
FRESHLY MILLED BLACK PEPPER TO TASTE

Drain the tomatoes, reserving their juice. Strain the captured juice to hold back the seeds. Using your fingers, push out the excess seeds from each tomato. Using your hands, a fork, or a potato masher, crush or mash the tomatoes. Set the tomatoes and juice aside.

In a saucepan over medium-low heat, melt 4 tablespoons of the butter. Add the onion, celery, carrot, and basil and sauté gently until the vegetables are quite soft but not browned, 10 to 12 minutes. Add the tomato paste and stir to blend with the vegetables. Add the tomatoes and their juice and the wine. Simmer over low heat, stirring frequently, until a sauce consistency is formed, about 45 minutes. Remove the pan from the heat.

When the sauce has cooled somewhat, position a food mill over a clean saucepan and pass the sauce through it, being sure to press out as much pulp as possible. Place over medium heat just long enough for the sauce to heat through, about 3 minutes. Season to taste with salt and pepper. Remove from the heat and stir in the remaining 2 tablespoons butter.

YIELD: Makes approximately 2½ cups. Two cups are sufficient for saucing 1 pound of pasta.

AHEAD-OF-TIME NOTE: This sauce can be made 3 or 4 days in advance of using and stored tightly covered in the refrigerator, or it can be frozen for up to 3 months. Whether storing it in the refrigerator or freezer, leave out the pepper and the remaining 2 tablespoons butter. Stir them into the sauce after reheating.

Salsa di pomodoro e olive nere
TOMATO SAUCE WITH GARLIC AND BLACK OLIVES

Olives and tomatoes have a great affinity for each other in sauces both raw and cooked. I am very fond of this sauce because it is both delicious and versatile. Of course, it is ideal with pasta, for both spaghetti and macaroni cuts. I like to use it on pizza, too, and as a condiment for fish. Remember, the bland, canned olive varieties are never suitable in Italian dishes, and certainly this sauce recipe is no exception. While only a few olives are included, they are tasty enough to flavor the sauce; a larger quantity would take over. If you wish to use the sauce for pizza, you can double the amount of olives, then smear the sauce over the uncooked pizza disk before baking.

3 TABLESPOONS EXTRA-VIRGIN OLIVE OIL

1 LARGE CLOVE GARLIC, MINCED

2 TABLESPOONS MINCED YELLOW ONION

3 TABLESPOONS TOMATO PASTE

2 TABLESPOONS SHARPLY FLAVORED IMPORTED BLACK OLIVES SUCH AS GAETA, NIÇOISE, OR KALAMATA, PITTED AND SLICED

2 TABLESPOONS CHOPPED FRESH ITALIAN PARSLEY

1 TEASPOON CHOPPED FRESH MARJORAM, OR 1/2 TEASPOON DRIED MARJORAM

2 1/2 CUPS CRUSHED, CANNED PLUM TOMATOES

1/2 TEASPOON SALT

3/4 CUP WATER

Combine 2 tablespoons of the olive oil, the garlic, and onion in a cold saucepan. Place over medium-low heat and sauté gently until the garlic and onion begin to color, 4 to 5 minutes. Stir in the tomato paste and cook gently for 2 to 3 minutes. Stir in the olives, parsley, and marjoram, and then the tomatoes, salt, and water. Cover partially and allow the sauce to simmer gently, stirring occasionally, until it thickens, about 20 minutes.

Remove from the heat and stir in the remaining 1 tablespoon extra-virgin olive oil.

YIELD: Makes approximately 2 1/2 cups. Two cups are sufficient for saucing 1 pound of pasta.

AHEAD-OF-TIME NOTE: This sauce can be made 3 or 4 days in advance of using and stored tightly covered in the refrigerator, or it can be frozen for up to 3 months. Whether storing it in the refrigerator or freezer, leave out the remaining 1 tablespoon olive oil. Stir it into the sauce after reheating.

Salsa di pomodoro con cipolla e rosmarino
TOMATO SAUCE WITH ONION AND ROSEMARY

This unusual tomato sauce is pink rather than a deep tomato color because it consists primarily of onions. It is exceedingly sweet and delicate, and a good choice for fresh pasta or dried egg noodles; it is also an excellent accompaniment to roasted pork, chicken, or fish. The onions must be sliced very thinly and then cooked very slowly so that they become creamy as they cook.

3 TABLESPOONS UNSALTED BUTTER

3 TABLESPOONS EXTRA-VIRGIN OLIVE OIL

3 LARGE YELLOW ONIONS, QUARTERED AND SLICED
  PAPER-THIN

1/4 CUP PLUS 6 TABLESPOONS HOT TAP WATER, OR AS
  NEEDED

2 TABLESPOONS TOMATO PASTE

1 TEASPOON FINELY CHOPPED FRESH ROSEMARY, OR 1/2
  TEASPOON CRUMBLED DRIED ROSEMARY

1 1/4 TEASPOONS SALT

1/4 TEASPOON FRESHLY MILLED WHITE OR BLACK
  PEPPER

In a saucepan over high heat, melt the butter with the olive oil. When it is hot enough to make the onions sizzle, add them and sauté for 3 minutes, stirring frequently. Take care not to allow them to color. Immediately reduce the heat to medium-low, cover, and continue to cook the onions for 5 minutes; stir them occasionally, but always replace the lid. Add the 1/4 cup hot water, cover again, and continue to cook over the gentlest possible heat for 30 minutes, gradually adding the remaining 6 tablespoons hot water during this time, and replacing the cover each time after you do. The onions should become very soft.

Stir in the tomato paste, the rosemary, salt, and pepper, and an additional tablespoon or two of hot water if necessary. Whether you need additional water will depend on how much liquid the onions have thrown off. Keep in mind that you want the sauce to be smooth: not too dry, but not too loose. Cover and cook over very gentle heat, stirring occasionally, for an additional 15 minutes, or until a nice consistency is achieved.

YIELD: Makes approximately 2 cups. This recipe is sufficient for saucing 1 pound of pasta.

AHEAD-OF-TIME NOTE: The sauce can be made 3 to 4 days in advance of using and stored tightly covered in the refrigerator.

Pesto di pomodoro
SUN-DRIED TOMATO PESTO

Tomatoes are dried in the sun as a way of preserving them after the harvest. They are not meant to be eaten whole, as they are leathery and the flavor too concentrated to be enjoyable alone. They are rather typically used in sauces, stuffings, soups, and stews. In this recipe, a *pesto* of sorts, the raw (uncooked) fragrance and flavor of the olive oil is fully experienced. A tablespoon of this gives a delicious boost to soups, stews, and certain tomato sauces where such a pungent flavor would be appropriate. The *pesto* can also be combined with spaghetti or *spaghettini*—never fresh pasta—but *be sure to underdrain it* when tossing it with this unctuous *pesto,* and to reserve approximately a cup of the pasta cooking water, should you need to add more moisture after tossing. The spaghetti or *spaghettini* must be dripping wet because the dried tomatoes do not impart enough moisture to the sauce. Thus the cooking water becomes part of the sauce. To store the *pesto,* cover with olive oil and refrigerate for up to a month, but leave out the cheese and parsley until you are ready to use it.

1 CUP FIRMLY PACKED, DRAINED SUN-DRIED TOMATOES
   IN OIL, OR ¾ CUP DRY-PACKED SUN-DRIED TOMATOES

1 LARGE CLOVE GARLIC, MINCED

¼ CUP FINELY CHOPPED WHITE OR RED ONION

½ TEASPOON CHOPPED FRESH THYME, OR ¼ TEASPOON
   CRUMBLED DRIED THYME

¼ TEASPOON SALT, OR TO TASTE

PINCH OF RED PEPPER FLAKES

½ CUP EXTRA-VIRGIN OLIVE OIL

¼ CUP WATER

¼ CUP CHOPPED FRESH ITALIAN PARSLEY

2 TABLESPOONS FRESHLY GRATED PECORINO CHEESE

If using sun-dried tomatoes that have not been stored in oil, rehydrate them according to the directions on page 23 before proceeding. Using a sharp knife, cleaver, or mezzaluna, chop the tomatoes coarsely. Do not use a food processor or blender to chop here, or the ingredients will get mushy.

In a bowl, combine the chopped tomatoes, garlic, onion, thyme, salt, and red pepper flakes. Add the olive oil and mix thoroughly with a wooden spoon. Add the water, parsley, and cheese and stir until well combined. Use immediately, or store as directed in the recipe introduction.

YIELD: Makes approximately 1½ cups. This recipe is sufficient for saucing 1 pound of pasta.

CHAPTER FOUR

Ragù
Tomato and Meat Sauces

Salsa di pomodoro con fegatini di pollo
TOMATO SAUCE WITH CHICKEN LIVERS

Salsa di pomodoro, salsiccia e zafferano
TOMATO AND SAUSAGE SAUCE WITH SAFFRON

Salsa di pomodoro alla pugliese
APULIAN TOMATO SAUCE WITH LAMB

Ragù alla toscana
TUSCAN BEEF AND CHICKEN GIBLET SAUCE

Passato di pomodoro con prosciutto
SIEVED FRESH TOMATO SAUCE WITH BUTTER,
VEGETABLES, PROSCIUTTO, AND WHITE WINE

Salsa alla bolognese
TOMATO AND MEAT SAUCE, BOLOGNA STYLE

Ragù del mezzogiorno
SOUTHERN-STYLE MEAT SAUCE

Ragù alla sarda
SARDINIAN RAGÙ OF VEAL AND PORK

Ragù con funghi alla toscana
TUSCAN MEAT SAUCE WITH MUSHROOMS

Salsa di pomodoro con polpettine di carne
TOMATO SAUCE WITH LITTLE MEATBALLS

Salsa di pomodoro con rosmarino e ossa di arrosto
TOMATO SAUCE MADE WITH ROSEMARY AND
LEFTOVER BONES FROM A ROAST

*R*agù are hearty, flavorful meat sauces that always begin with a *soffritto* of garlic or onion (or both) and oil or butter (or both) and possibly finely chopped carrots, celery, and parsley. (The use of lard has largely waned.) Wine adds depth and its own unique flavor. The vegetable mixture adds body to the sauce, sweetens and refines. Unlike other tomato sauces, *ragù* are cooked for an exceptionally long time. This is both to tenderize economy cuts of meat when they are included, and to achieve a complex, rich-tasting sauce. In contrast to simple tomato sauces where clarity of flavor and freshness is the object, the components of *ragù*, after a complex cooking process, are designed to merge into a sauce that has its own characteristic flavor. The tomatoes and other ingredients are just a road to the end result. Such lengthy cooking seems contradictory to the general principles of brief cooking of tomato sauces, but what we're after in *ragù* are rich, complex flavors where tomatoes only play a part.

As I pointed out in my history of tomato sauce at the outset of this book, the *ragù* of the colder northern Italian regions tend to be cooked far longer than those of the warmer southern ones. A *ragù alla bolognese* would never cook for less than four hours (a century ago, six hours was standard), while a southern meat sauce might cook for as little as an hour. What saves the sauce from the bitterness that can result from cooking tomatoes too long is that *ragù* are always cooked over very gentle heat.

While the *ragù* of central and northern Italy include finely diced or minced meats, those of the south are usually made with whole pieces of stewing meat, such as the shoulder, neck, or shank. The latter has traditionally provided an economical solution to feeding a family: The sauce is served with pasta as a first course, and the meat is eaten as a second course.

Other sauces in this chapter contain meat but they are not long-simmered ones, and some call for only a small amount of meat. But even the most restrained addition of tasty *prosciutto crudo* can convey the satisfactions of a meat sauce, and the sauce can be prepared relatively quickly.

Salsa di pomodoro con fegatini di pollo
TOMATO SAUCE WITH CHICKEN LIVERS

Chicken livers must be very fresh, plump, and firm in order to be good. The best-tasting livers are from organic or free-range birds that have not been exposed to antibiotics, growth stimulants, or other unnatural additives in their diets. Any livers that are discolored or spongy should be discarded. This delicate butter-based sauce is suitable for spaghetti, *linguine*, or egg noodles; it is also lovely with *polenta* or rice. For any of these dishes, pass freshly grated *parmigiano* at the table.

10 OUNCES VERY FRESH CHICKEN LIVERS

1½ CUPS CANNED, PEELED PLUM TOMATOES IN JUICE

4 TABLESPOONS UNSALTED BUTTER

2 TABLESPOONS OLIVE OIL

2 CLOVES GARLIC, BRUISED

1 MEDIUM-SIZED YELLOW ONION, FINELY CHOPPED

1 TEASPOON FRESH ROSEMARY LEAVES, OR ½ TEA-
SPOON DRIED ROSEMARY

2 TABLESPOONS TOMATO PASTE

½ CUP GOOD-QUALITY DRY RED WINE

½ TEASPOON SALT, OR TO TASTE

FRESHLY MILLED BLACK PEPPER TO TASTE

Wash the livers and remove any fat, membranes, green spots, and other discolorations. Bring a saucepan three-fourths full of water to a rapid boil. Add the chicken livers and blanch for 1 minute. Drain and immediately rinse in cold water. Allow the livers to cool completely: place them in the freezer until firm, about 1 hour, or refrigerate for several hours or overnight. Then cut them into quarters.

Drain the tomatoes, reserving their juice for another use. Using your fingers, push out the excess seeds from each tomato. Coarsely chop the tomatoes and set aside.

In a saucepan over medium-low heat, melt the butter with the olive oil. Add the garlic and sauté until golden, 1 to 2 minutes. Remove and discard the garlic.

Raise the heat to medium, add the livers and onion to the pan, and sauté until the livers are golden on the outside but still pink on the inside, about 3 minutes. Transfer the livers to a bowl but leave the onion in the pan.

Crush the fresh or dried rosemary leaves in your hand to release some of the oils and add to the pan along with the tomato paste. Cook for 1 minute, then stir in the tomatoes, wine, salt, and pepper. Cook gently until the alcohol evaporates, about 3 minutes. Return the livers to the pan and heat gently for 2 minutes, then serve.

YIELD: Makes approximately 1¼ cups. One cup is sufficient for saucing ½ pound of pasta.

AHEAD-OF-TIME NOTE: This sauce can be made 3 or 4 days in advance of using and stored tightly covered in the refrigerator.

Salsa di pomodoro, salsiccia e zafferano
TOMATO AND SAUSAGE SAUCE WITH SAFFRON

It is characteristic of Sardinian cooking to add saffron to sauces, as in this recipe. Not only does the saffron add lovely flavor, but it also imparts a deep golden cast to the red of the tomato. This sauce is traditionally served with *malloreddus*, a pasta peculiar to the island. Substitute *cavatelli* or factory-made *gnocchetti*, similar to *conchiglie* (shells). It can also be served with *polenta* or rice. Pass freshly grated *pecorino* or *parmigiano* at the table with the sauce.

2½ CUPS CANNED, PEELED PLUM TOMATOES IN PURÉE,
   OR 2½ CUPS CANNED, PEELED PLUM TOMATOES IN
   JUICE PLUS 3 TABLESPOONS TOMATO PASTE
1 TABLESPOON OLIVE OIL
1 LARGE RED OR YELLOW ONION, FINELY CHOPPED
1 POUND SWEET FENNEL-FLAVORED ITALIAN SAUSAGE
   MEAT
2 ENVELOPES (⅛ TEASPOON TOTAL) SAFFRON POWDER,
   OR ⅛ TEASPOON SAFFRON THREADS
SALT TO TASTE

Drain the tomatoes, reserving their juice or purée. Strain the captured juice or purée to hold back the seeds. Using your fingers, push out the excess seeds from each tomato. Chop the tomatoes and set aside with their juice or purée.

In a saucepan over medium-low heat, warm the olive oil. Add the onion and sauté until softened, 8 to 10 minutes. Add the sausage meat and sauté gently until the meat has browned but not hardened, 5 to 7 minutes.

If using tomato purée, simply stir in the chopped tomatoes and purée. If using tomato paste, first add the paste and stir, then add the chopped tomatoes and their juice. If using saffron threads, heat them gently in a small pan on the stove top for 1 minute. Then crush them between your fingers and stir them into the sauce. If using saffron powder, simply stir it into the sauce. Add the salt and simmer gently, uncovered, over medium-low heat, until a thick consistency forms, about 25 minutes. Stir the sauce occasionally as it cooks. Taste and adjust for salt just before serving.

YIELD: Makes approximately 2¾ cups. Two cups are sufficient for saucing 1 pound of pasta.

AHEAD-OF-TIME NOTE: This sauce can be made 4 or 5 days in advance of using and stored tightly covered in the refrigerator, or it can be frozen for up to 3 months.

Salsa di pomodoro alla pugliese
APULIAN TOMATO SAUCE WITH LAMB

This *ragù* is one of the signature dishes of the region of Apulia, located in the heel of the Italian "boot." It was traditionally made with *agnellone*, aged lamb or mutton, which gives the sauce a very gamy flavor. My friend and colleague Anna Amendolara Nurse, who is of Apulian stock, gave me this version, which is how her mother, Rosa Amendolara, made it. Lamb shanks are used rather than mutton. The *ragù*, crowning a platter full of homemade *orecchiette* (little pasta ears) and followed by roasted rabbit, is an Apulian Easter tradition. Macaroni cuts that are traditionally combined with this sauce include short or long *ziti*. Grated *pecorino*, sheep's cheese, is passed at the table to top the pasta.

6 CUPS CANNED, PEELED PLUM TOMATOES IN JUICE

1/2 CUP OLIVE OIL

4 VERY FRESH, PINK, FAT, AND MEATY LAMB SHANKS
  (1 TO 1 1/4 POUNDS EACH)

4 CLOVES GARLIC, BRUISED

1 LARGE YELLOW ONION, CHOPPED

3/4 CUP GOOD-QUALITY DRY RED WINE

3/4 CUP TOMATO PASTE

1 TEASPOON SALT, OR TO TASTE

RED PEPPER FLAKES TO TASTE

5 LARGE FRESH BASIL LEAVES

Pass the tomatoes and their juices through a food mill directly into a pot large enough to accommodate the shanks later. Bring to a boil, then reduce the heat so the tomatoes simmer.

In a skillet large enough to accommodate the lamb shanks comfortably, heat the olive oil over medium-high heat. When it is hot enough to make the shanks sizzle, add them and brown on all sides, turning when necessary to color them evenly, about 15 minutes. Transfer the browned lamb to the pot with the tomatoes. Drain off all but 1/3 cup oil from the skillet.

Add the garlic to the oil in the skillet and sauté over medium-low heat until it is golden, 1 or 2 minutes. Scoop the garlic cloves out and add them to the tomatoes. Add the onion to the oil and sauté over medium-low heat until it is softened and golden, 10 to 15 minutes. Increase the heat to medium, then pour in the wine and allow it to evaporate, about 3 minutes. Add the tomato paste to the onion, using a wooden spoon to stir and dislodge any bits of meat that are stuck to the bottom of the pan. Sauté for 5 minutes to marry the flavors.

Add the onion mixture, salt, and red pepper flakes to the simmering tomatoes and lamb and stir well. Cover partially and simmer, stirring occasionally, until the meat is tender but not falling from the bones, no longer than 1 1/2 hours. Keep an eye on the heat to be sure the sauce bubbles gently and steadily as it simmers; it should not bubble violently. Stir in the basil. Check and adjust for salt.

Serve the sauce hot with cooked, drained macaroni. Offer the meat as a side dish with the pasta, or as a second course.

YIELD: Makes approximately 8 cups. Two cups are sufficient for saucing 1 pound of pasta.

AHEAD-OF-TIME NOTE: This sauce can be made 4 or 5 days in advance of using and stored tightly covered in the refrigerator, or it can be frozen for up to 3 months. Whether refrigerating or freezing the sauce, keep the shanks—bones and all—immersed in the sauce and reheat them together. Nibbling on the succulent shank bones after the meat has been stripped off is part of the enjoyment of the *ragù*.

Ragù alla toscana
TUSCAN BEEF AND CHICKEN GIBLET SAUCE

The use of chicken innards makes this sauce typically Tuscan. Chicken gizzards, hearts, cockscombs, livers, and intestines (the latter first soaked in water and vinegar and then carefully washed) give a great flavor boost to a tomato-and-meat sauce. Unfortunately, some of these chicken parts are typically eschewed in America and are largely unavailable, except for livers and gizzards. The latter (sometimes known simply as giblets) are added to this sauce, which is then fortified with dry red wine and cooked very gently for a long time. The result is a rich-tasting, complex *ragù*. In and around Siena, it is typically served over *pici*, handmade knitting-needle-like pasta; throughout Tuscany, it is used as a sauce for *cannelloni* and for sturdy macaroni cuts such as *gemelli* (twins), *creste di gallo* (cockscombs), or *ziti*, and with *polenta* dishes or with *risotto bianco*, simple white *risotto*.

2½ CUPS CANNED, PEELED PLUM TOMATOES IN JUICE;
   2½ POUNDS FRESH, SWEET, MATURE VINE-RIPENED
   TOMATOES; OR 2½ CUPS CANNED, CRUSHED PLUM
   TOMATOES
½ POUND CHICKEN GIZZARDS
4 TABLESPOONS EXTRA-VIRGIN OLIVE OIL
1 MEDIUM-SIZED YELLOW ONION, CHOPPED
1 LARGE CARROT, SCRAPED AND CHOPPED
1 MEDIUM CELERY STALK, INCLUDING LEAVES, CHOPPED
2 TABLESPOONS CHOPPED FRESH ITALIAN PARSLEY
½ POUND GROUND LEAN BEEF, OR A MIXTURE OF BEEF
   AND PORK
½ CUP GOOD-QUALITY DRY RED WINE
1 TEASPOON SALT
2 TABLESPOONS TOMATO PASTE
FRESHLY MILLED BLACK OR WHITE PEPPER TO TASTE

If using canned tomatoes, drain them, reserving their juice. Strain the captured juice to hold back the seeds. Using your fingers, push out the excess seeds, then chop the tomatoes and set the tomatoes and juice aside. If using fresh tomatoes, slip them into a saucepan of rapidly boiling water and blanch for 30 to 45 seconds. Drain the tomatoes and immediately plunge them into cold water. Drain again and, using a paring knife, lift off the skins and cut out the tough core portions. Cut into quarters lengthwise and, using your fingers, push out the excess seeds. Chop the tomatoes and set aside. If using crushed tomatoes, reserve.

To clean the gizzards, wash them and pat dry with a clean kitchen towel. Using a sharp knife, slice away the tough outer, whitish skin from each pair of gizzards, then slice them thinly and set aside. In a saucepan over medium-low heat, warm the olive oil. Add the onion, carrot, celery, and parsley, and sauté gently, stirring occasionally, until the vegetables have softened, about 15 minutes. Raise the heat to medium and add the gizzards; sauté for 5 minutes, and then add the ground meat. Reduce the heat to medium-low and using a wooden spoon, break up the meat and stir it to brown evenly. It should turn light brown; do not allow it to harden. Add the wine and allow the alcohol to evaporate, about 3 minutes.

Stir in the salt, tomato paste, and the tomatoes and juice or crushed tomatoes. Allow the sauce to come to a bubbly simmer, then turn the heat down to as low as possible and partially cover the saucepan. Continue to simmer, always over the lowest possible heat and stirring occasionally, until the sauce is thick and pebbly (the Tuscans actually call this *ragù, la ghiaiosa,* "the pebbly sauce"), about 1½ hours.

YIELD: Makes approximately 5 cups. Two cups are sufficient for saucing 1 pound of pasta.

AHEAD-OF-TIME NOTE: This sauce can be made 4 or 5 days in advance of using and stored tightly covered in the refrigerator, or it can be frozen for up to 3 months.

Passato di pomodoro con prosciutto
SIEVED FRESH TOMATO SAUCE WITH BUTTER, VEGETABLES, PROSCIUTTO, AND WHITE WINE

Prosciutto imparts subtle flavor to this delicate sauce (*prosciutto crudo* means that the ham is not preserved through cooking; rather, it is salted and air-cured), while butter and white wine give it a refinement that heartier sauces lack. I like to make it when good vine-ripened tomatoes are at hand because they, too, contribute to a more delicately flavored sauce. Good canned tomatoes can also be used, however.

The variation with hazelnuts and lemon peel is a particularly suitable sauce for potato *gnocchi*.

2½ POUNDS FRESH, SWEET, MATURE VINE-RIPENED
    TOMATOES, OR 2½ CUPS CANNED, PEELED PLUM
    TOMATOES IN JUICE
4 TABLESPOONS UNSALTED BUTTER
2 OUNCES PROSCIUTTO CRUDO, INCLUDING FAT, THINLY
    SLICED AND THEN CHOPPED
1 SMALL RED ONION, FINELY CHOPPED
1 MEDIUM CARROT, SCRAPED AND FINELY CHOPPED
1 MEDIUM CELERY STALK, INCLUDING LEAVES, FINELY
    CHOPPED
1 TABLESPOON CHOPPED FRESH ITALIAN PARSLEY
½ CUP GOOD-QUALITY DRY WHITE WINE
1½ TABLESPOONS TOMATO PASTE
½ TEASPOON SALT, OR TO TASTE
FRESHLY MILLED BLACK OR WHITE PEPPER TO TASTE.

If using fresh tomatoes, cut out the tough area around the core of each tomato. Cut the tomatoes crosswise and squeeze out any excess water. (Plum tomatoes are less likely to be excessively watery, but other varieties will be very weepy). Dice the tomatoes and place in a saucepan. If using canned tomatoes, using your hands, a fork, or a potato masher, crush or mash the tomatoes and transfer to a saucepan. Place the tomatoes over medium-low heat and cook uncovered, stirring occasionally, until a thick consistency is reached, 35 to 45 minutes. Remove from the heat.

When the tomatoes have cooled somewhat, pass them through a food mill, being sure to press out as much of the pulp as possible. (The water passes through the mill first and the bulk of the sauce is contained in the pulp that remains.)

Meanwhile, in a large saucepan or deep skillet over low heat, melt 3 tablespoons of the butter. Add the *prosciutto* and sauté gently for 2 to 3 minutes until it is lightly colored and the fat has melted. Add the onion, carrot, celery, and parsley, stirring to coat all the vegetables evenly with the butter. Sauté over low heat until the vegetables have softened and colored but not browned, 10 to 12 minutes. Add the wine little by little until it is all absorbed and the alcohol has evaporated; the wine should be dribbled in over about 2 minutes and it should take about 3 minutes to evaporate the alcohol. Stir in the tomato paste, distributing it well throughout the vegetable mixture. Then stir in the salt and sieved tomatoes. Cover partially and simmer over low heat, stirring occasionally, about 20 minutes. The sauce is done when the vegetables are softened completely and the sauce is thick.

Remove from the heat, check for salt, and then add the pepper and the remaining 1 tablespoon butter. Stir thoroughly before using.

YIELD: Makes approximately 3 cups. Two cups are sufficient for saucing 1 pound pasta.

VARIATION WITH HAZELNUTS AND LEMON: Blanch 2 lemon zest strips, each about 1-inch long and ½-inch wide, for 30 seconds, drain, and add with the tomato paste. Add ¼ cup skinned and chopped hazelnuts during the last 5 minutes of cooking.

AHEAD-OF-TIME NOTE: This sauce can be made 3 or 4 days in advance of using and stored tightly covered in the refrigerator, or it can be frozen for up to 3 months. Whether storing it in the refrigerator or freezer, leave out the pepper and remaining 1 tablespoon butter. Stir into the sauce after reheating.

Salsa alla bolognese
TOMATO AND MEAT SAUCE, BOLOGNA STYLE

Here is one of the many versions of the complex, fragrant, delicate meat sauce that is a classic of the region of Emilia-Romagna, the home of homemade egg pasta. Tomato is not the focus of this winey, creamy *ragù*; rather, it is a supporting ingredient. While I have listed ground beef in this recipe, a combination of veal, pork, and beef can be used for an even more refined sauce.

Salsa alla bolognese is typically used between layers in homemade *lasagne*, a signature dish of that region, and it is the classic sauce for another mythic Emilian food, fresh homemade *tagliatelle*. *Pappardelle* and *fettuccine* are also suitable matches. Among its other uses is as a finishing sauce for *costolette alla bolognese*, veal cutlets that are first breaded and sautéed in butter, and then covered with cheese, *prosciutto crudo*, and the *ragù* and baked. The creaminess of this luscious sauce also makes it well suited to some macaroni cuts, both because they are sturdy enough to support its creamy texture (a result of the very slow evaporation during lengthy cooking and the addition of milk to the sauce), and because the meat is cradled within the curves of the pasta. The most compatible macaroni cuts are *fusilli corti* (short twists), *gnocchetti*, and *rigatoni*. Pass freshly grated *parmigiano* at the table.

2½ CUPS CANNED, PEELED PLUM TOMATOES IN JUICE

3 TABLESPOONS UNSALTED BUTTER

1 TABLESPOON EXTRA-VIRGIN OLIVE OIL

1 SMALL WHITE OR YELLOW ONION, FINELY CHOPPED

1 SMALL CELERY STALK, INCLUDING LEAVES, FINELY
  CHOPPED

½ SMALL CARROT, SCRAPED AND FINELY CHOPPED

1 TABLESPOON CHOPPED FRESH ITALIAN PARSLEY

¾ POUND GOOD-QUALITY LEAN GROUND BEEF, PREFER-
  ABLY CHUCK

2 OUNCES PROSCIUTTO CRUDO, INCLUDING FAT, THINLY
  SLICED AND THEN CUT INTO JULIENNE STRIPS

½ TEASPOON SALT, OR TO TASTE

½ CUP GOOD-QUALITY DRY WHITE WINE

⅔ CUP MILK

⅛ TEASPOON NUTMEG, PREFERABLY FRESHLY GRATED

FRESHLY MILLED WHITE OR BLACK PEPPER TO TASTE

Drain the tomatoes, reserving their juice. Strain the captured juice to hold back the seeds. Using your fingers, push out the excess seeds from each tomato. Chop the tomatoes and set the tomatoes and juice aside.

In a large, wide Dutch oven or large, deep skillet, melt 2 tablespoons of the butter with the olive oil over low heat. Stir in the onion, celery, carrot, and parsley and sauté over low heat until the vegetables are quite soft but not at all browned, about 12 minutes. Keeping the heat very low, add the ground meat and *prosciutto*. The meat must heat very gently, only enough to color it lightly on the outside; preventing it from hardening allows it to absorb the flavors of the other ingredients and to become delicate and creamy. Stir in the salt and wine. Simmer very gently for several minutes until the alcohol evaporates and the liquid begins to be absorbed by the meat and vegetables.

Now add the milk and nutmeg. (It is important to add the milk before adding the tomatoes so that it will be absorbed by the meat.) Simmer gently for 10 minutes, then add the tomatoes and juice. As soon as the sauce begins to simmer, turn the heat down as low as possible; if your burner cannot be regulated to a setting that is low enough, insert a flame tamer between the burner and the pan. Cover partially and continue to simmer, always over the lowest possible heat and stirring occasionally, for about 4 hours. When the sauce is finished, stir in the remaining 1 tablespoon butter and the pepper. Check and adjust for salt.

YIELD: Makes approximately 2 cups. This recipe is sufficient for saucing 1 pound of pasta.

AHEAD-OF-TIME NOTE: This sauce can be made 3 or 4 days in advance of using and stored tightly covered in the refrigerator or it can be frozen for up to 3 months. Whether storing it in the refrigerator, or freezer, leave out the remaining 1 tablespoon butter and the pepper. Stir them in after reheating the sauce.

Ragù del mezzogiorno
SOUTHERN-STYLE MEAT SAUCE

This dense, richly flavored sauce is a traditional *ragù* of the Italian south, typically served with dried pasta such as spaghetti or *linguine*, or macaroni cuts, including *rigatoni, ziti, cavatelli,* or *creste di gallo.*

3 CUPS CANNED, PEELED PLUM TOMATOES IN JUICE

1 POUND BEEF CHUCK STEAK, IN ONE PIECE

1/2 POUND PORK SHOULDER, IN ONE PIECE, OR 1 LARGE PORK CHOP WITH BONE

3 TABLESPOONS EXTRA-VIRGIN OLIVE OIL

1 CLOVE GARLIC, BRUISED

1 MEDIUM-SIZED RED ONION, MINCED

1 SMALL CARROT, SCRAPED AND MINCED

1 SMALL CELERY STALK, MINCED

1/2 CUP TOMATO PASTE

1/2 CUP GOOD-QUALITY DRY RED WINE

SALT TO TASTE

FRESHLY MILLED BLACK PEPPER TO TASTE

3/4 CUP WATER

1 TEASPOON CHOPPED FRESH BASIL

Drain the tomatoes, reserving their juice. Strain the captured juice to remove the seeds. Using your fingers, push out the excess seeds from each tomato. Chop the tomatoes and set the tomatoes and juice aside.

Trim all the fat from the chuck steak and pork, but leave each meat in one piece. In a Dutch oven or other heavy pot over medium-high heat, warm the olive oil and brown the meats on all sides, about 12 minutes. Remove the meats to a plate and set aside. Reduce the heat to medium-low, add the garlic, and sauté until golden, 1 to 2 minutes. Remove and discard the garlic. Add the onion, carrot, and celery to the pot and sauté, still over medium-low heat, until the vegetables are softened, about 10 minutes. Stir in the tomato paste and sauté for 3 minutes. Then return the meat (and any juices that have collected on the plate) to the pot and add the wine. Simmer, uncovered, to evaporate the alcohol, about 3 minutes.

Add the tomatoes and juice and season with salt and pepper. Add the water and basil and bring to a boil. Immediately reduce the heat to low, cover partially, and simmer, stirring now and then, until the meat is thoroughly tender and the sauce has thickened, about 1 3/4 hours.

For a rustic sauce, serve the sauce unsieved. For a smooth sauce, remove the meat and pass the sauce through a food mill. A food processor will make a slightly thicker sauce, since it doesn't actually strain any part of it. Serve the sauce over pasta; slice the meat and serve it alongside the pasta.

YIELD: Makes approximately 2 1/2 cups. Two cups are sufficient for saucing 1 pound of pasta.

AHEAD-OF-TIME NOTE: This sauce can be made 3 or 4 days in advance of using and stored tightly covered in the refrigerator, or it can be frozen for up to 3 months.

Ragù alla sarda
SARDINIAN RAGÙ OF VEAL AND PORK

Here is a lovely Sardinian *ragù* that is often served with a kind of *polenta* made from semolina flour. The sauce is suitable for many types of dried pasta, including spaghetti and medium-sized macaroni varieties. Serve with freshly grated *pecorino* or *parmigiano* cheese at the table.

2½ CUPS CANNED, PEELED PLUM TOMATOES IN JUICE

2 OUNCES PANCETTA, THINLY SLICED, OR 3 STRIPS LEAN BACON

2 TABLESPOONS OLIVE OIL

1 LARGE RED OR YELLOW ONION, FINELY CHOPPED

½ POUND GROUND LEAN PORK

½ POUND GROUND VEAL

3 TABLESPOONS CHOPPED FRESH ITALIAN PARSLEY

SMALL HANDFUL OF FRESH BASIL LEAVES, CHOPPED

1 TEASPOON CHOPPED FRESH SAGE, OR ½ TEASPOON CRUMBLED DRIED SAGE

¼ CUP TOMATO PASTE

½ CUP GOOD-QUALITY DRY WHITE WINE OR WATER

SALT TO TASTE

FRESHLY MILLED BLACK PEPPER TO TASTE

Drain the tomatoes, reserving their juice. Strain the captured juice to hold back the seeds. Using your fingers, push out the excess seeds from each tomato. Chop the tomatoes and set the tomatoes and juice aside. If using pancetta, chop it finely. If using bacon, drop it into boiling water to cover and blanch for 30 seconds. Drain, rinse in cold water, and drain again. Chop finely.

In a saucepan over medium heat, warm the olive oil. Add the onion. Sauté the onion until it is translucent, about 3 minutes. Add the pancetta or bacon; reduce the heat to medium-low and sauté until the onion is totally softened and the *pancetta* or bacon has colored, about 8 minutes or so. Add the ground meats, parsley, basil, and sage and sauté until the meat is colored but not hard, about 2 minutes. Add the tomatoes and juice and the tomato paste. Stir well and simmer, still over medium-low heat, for 5 minutes; then stir in the wine or water. Cover partially and simmer over the gentlest possible heat until the liquid thrown off by the tomatoes is evaporated and a thick sauce is formed, about 1 hour, adding water if necessary to prevent the sauce from becoming dry. Season with salt and pepper.

YIELD: Makes approximately 6 cups. Two cups are sufficient for saucing 1 pound of pasta.

AHEAD-OF-TIME NOTE: This sauce can be made up to 4 days in advance of using and stored tightly covered in the refrigerator, or it can be frozen for up to 3 months.

Ragù con funghi alla toscana
TUSCAN MEAT SAUCE WITH MUSHROOMS

This rich-tasting sauce is ideal for *lasagne*, and a natural for virtually any dried pasta cut (no thinner than spaghetti, though). It is also a lovely sauce served alongside or folded into a simple *risotto*, and a wonderful accompaniment to *polenta*. Serve the sauce with *pecorino* or *parmigiano* cheese.

¼ OUNCE DRIED PORCINI MUSHROOMS

¼ CUP HOT TAP WATER

2½ CUPS CANNED, PEELED PLUM TOMATOES IN JUICE

2 TABLESPOONS UNSALTED BUTTER

2 TABLESPOONS OLIVE OIL

2 TABLESPOONS CHOPPED FRESH ITALIAN PARSLEY

1 MEDIUM CARROT, SCRAPED AND FINELY CHOPPED

1 MEDIUM CELERY STALK, INCLUDING LEAVES, FINELY CHOPPED

1 SMALL YELLOW ONION, FINELY CHOPPED

1 TEASPOON CHOPPED FRESH SAGE, OR ½ TEASPOON CRUMBLED DRIED SAGE

¾ POUND GROUND LEAN BEEF, OR A MIXTURE OF BEEF AND PORK

2 TABLESPOONS TOMATO PASTE

½ CUP GOOD-QUALITY DRY RED WINE

1 TEASPOON SALT, OR TO TASTE

¼ TEASPOON FRESHLY MILLED BLACK PEPPER, OR TO TASTE

In a small bowl, place the dried *porcini* in the hot water and let stand for 30 to 40 minutes. Remove the *porcini* from the liquid and rinse them under cold tap water to remove any sand or grit. Squeeze out the excess water and chop the mushrooms coarsely. Set aside. Strain the mushroom liquid through a cheesecloth-lined sieve (or use a paper towel). Set aside.

Meanwhile, drain the tomatoes, reserving their juice. Strain the captured juice to hold back the seeds. Using your fingers, push out the excess seeds from each tomato. Chop the tomatoes and set the tomatoes and their juice aside.

In a saucepan over medium-low heat, melt the butter with the olive oil. Add the parsley, carrot, celery, onion, and sage. Sauté over medium-low heat until the vegetables are softened, 10 to 12 minutes. Stir in the ground beef (or beef and pork) and sauté until colored but still somewhat pink inside, about 8 minutes. Take care not to overcook the meat.

Now stir in the chopped mushrooms, tomato paste, the reserved mushroom liquid, and the wine.

Simmer over low heat for 5 minutes to evaporate the alcohol. Add the tomatoes and juice, salt, and pepper. Cover partially and simmer until a thick, fragrant sauce forms, about 30 minutes.

YIELD: Makes approximately 5¼ cups. Two cups are sufficient for saucing 1 pound of pasta.

VARIATION WITH SAUSAGE: Substitute ¾ pound lean, sweet fennel-flavored Italian sausage meat for the ground meat(s).

AHEAD-OF-TIME NOTE: This sauce can be made 4 or 5 days in advance of using and stored tightly covered in the refrigerator, or it can be frozen for up to 3 months.

Salsa di pomodoro con polpettine di carne
TOMATO SAUCE WITH LITTLE MEATBALLS

This recipe is not actually a *ragù*, nor is it really Italian. The tomato-and-meatball sauce of the American-Italian kitchen is a hybrid. This is not to say that meatballs are not found on the Italian table. Called *crochette di carne* (meat croquettes) or *polpette*, among other things, they are typically served as *antipasti* or poached in broth. They are usually made from leftover cooked meat rather than raw minced meat, however, as the Italians don't consider grinding a good use of first-quality meat. Neither have I seen the meatball mated with tomato sauce for anointing pasta in Italy. But since spaghetti and meatballs have become an American institution, I happily offer my own recipe for this New World dish. The delicious meatballs that follow are from Sardinia (ergo the *pecorino*, sheep's cheese), where they are served in an aromatic meat-and-fowl broth on festive occasions. But they are perfectly content to simmer in the fruity tomato sauce offered here, or in any of the basic tomato sauces in chapter 1.

When made with a combination of beef, veal, and pork, these little meatballs are especially delicate. They can, however, be made entirely from beef with excellent results. The addition of mashed potato makes the meatballs light and moist rather than hard and dry. The sauce is given a lovely texture by the grated carrots and a pleasant natural sweetness by both the carrots and the large quantity of fresh basil. The sauce, combined with the meatballs, is a good choice for medium macaroni cuts, such as *conchiglie* (shells), *rigatoni*, and *pennette*. In this case, grated *parmigiano* or *parmigiano* combined with *pecorino* should be passed with the pasta at the table. But without the meatballs, the sauce is tremendously versatile, performing as a marvelous accompaniment to fish, eggs, poultry, or meat, as well as to southern-style baked *lasagne* dishes or other baked macaroni dishes. Alternatively, the meatballs can be cooked in a double recipe of Light Puréed Tomato Sauce (page 43).

For the sauce:
5 CUPS CANNED, PEELED PLUM TOMATOES IN PURÉE, OR
  5 CUPS CANNED, PEELED PLUM TOMATOES IN JUICE
  PLUS 4 TABLESPOONS TOMATO PASTE
1/2 CUP OLIVE OIL
2 MEDIUM CARROTS, SCRAPED AND GRATED
1 MEDIUM-SIZED YELLOW ONION, FINELY CHOPPED
1/2 CUP COARSELY CHOPPED FRESH BASIL
2 TEASPOONS SALT
1/2 CUP WATER

For the meatballs:
1/4 POUND STURDY SUGARLESS WHITE ITALIAN OR
  PEASANT BREAD, CRUSTS REMOVED
1/2 CUP MILK, OR MEAT BROTH OR STOCK
1 MEDIUM-SIZED BOILING POTATO, BOILED, PEELED,
  AND MASHED
1 1/4 POUNDS GROUND LEAN BEEF
1 1/4 POUNDS GROUND VEAL
1 EGG, BEATEN
1 MEDIUM-SIZED YELLOW ONION, GRATED
2 TABLESPOONS CHOPPED FRESH ITALIAN PARSLEY

1/4 CUP FRESHLY GRATED PECORINO CHEESE

OLIVE OIL FOR FRYING
1 TEASPOON SALT
1/2 TEASPOON FRESHLY MILLED BLACK OR WHITE
  PEPPER, OR TO TASTE

First prepare the sauce: Drain the tomatoes in purée or in juice, reserving the liquid. Strain the captured liquid to hold back the seeds. Using your fingers, push out the excess seeds from each tomato. Chop the tomatoes and set the tomatoes and purée or juice aside.

In a Dutch oven or other heavy pan over medium-low heat, warm the olive oil. Add the carrots and onion and stir to combine the vegetables with the oil. Cover and cook over low heat for 10 minutes, removing the cover only to stir occasionally. The vegetables should soften but not brown.

Meanwhile, in a food processor or in batches in a blender, combine the tomatoes and purée (or the tomatoes, juice, and tomato paste), the basil, and salt. Engage the processor or blender for several seconds to purée.

Add the puréed tomatoes and the water to the pot with the carrots and onion and bring to a boil. Immediately reduce the heat to low or medium-low so the sauce is at a simmer. Cook uncovered, stirring occasionally to prevent the sauce from burning on the pot bottom, until the sauce thickens, about 25 minutes. When the sauce is done, set it aside.

While the sauce is simmering, make the meatballs: In a bowl, soak the bread in the milk until softened, about 1 minute (or longer if the bread is stale). Squeeze well to wring out as much liquid as possible. In another bowl, combine the soaked bread with all the remaining meatball ingredients. Using your hands, form the mixture into little balls about the size of walnuts. In a large, deep skillet, pour in enough oil to reach halfway up the sides of the meatballs once they are added to the pan. Place over medium-high heat. When the oil is hot enough to make the meatballs sizzle, slip the meatballs into the oil, working in batches and leaving enough room around each to prevent crowding. If the meatballs are touching, they will steam rather than fry, and thus not cook properly. Sauté the meatballs in the sizzling oil, turning to color evenly, until they are lightly browned all over but not cooked through, about 8 minutes. When they are ready, transfer the meatballs to a platter lined with paper towels to absorb the excess oil.

When all the meatballs have been browned, drain off the excess oil from the skillet but do not discard the bits of meat that cling to the pan bottom. Add a few tablespoons of the tomato sauce to the skillet and, using a wooden spoon, loosen the bits that are stuck to the bottom, stirring them together with the sauce. Add this bit of sauce and the meatballs to the pan of sauce. Cover partially and simmer gently over low heat until the meatballs are cooked through and the sauce is at serving temperature, about 20 minutes. Stir in the salt and pepper.

YIELD: Makes approximately 6 cups sauce and 40 small meatballs. Two cups is sufficient for saucing 1 pound of pasta; serve the meatballs atop the sauce.

AHEAD-OF-TIME NOTE: This sauce can be made 4 or 5 days in advance of using and stored tightly covered in the refrigerator, or it can be frozen for up to 3 months. Whether storing it in the refrigerator or freezer, keep the meatballs immersed in the sauce.

Salsa di pomodoro con rosmarino e ossa di arrosto
TOMATO SAUCE MADE WITH ROSEMARY AND LEFTOVER BONES FROM A ROAST

The leftover bones from a meat roast are a treasure to the cook for flavoring sauces such as this one. If there are any leftover drippings, defat them and add them, too. If the meat was flavored while roasting with rosemary, thyme, or other herbs compatible with tomatoes, so much the better, but be sure to adjust the amount of rosemary called for in the ingredients list. The plethora of vegetables in this sauce makes it fruity, chunky, and naturally sweet. It is ideal with all medium macaroni cuts, such as shells, *penne, fusilli, ziti, rigatoni, cavatelli, gnocchetti,* and *gnocchetti sardi.* Or serve it over ribbon and strand cuts no thinner than spaghetti, including *linguine, bucatini,* and *ziti lunghi* (long ziti), or with homemade potato *gnocchi.*

6 TABLESPOONS EXTRA-VIRGIN OLIVE OIL

2 LARGE CARROTS, SCRAPED AND CHOPPED

2 CELERY STALKS, INCLUDING LEAVES, CHOPPED

2 MEDIUM-SIZED YELLOW ONIONS, CHOPPED

3 LARGE CLOVES GARLIC, CHOPPED

4 TEASPOONS CHOPPED FRESH ROSEMARY, OR 2 TEA-
SPOONS CRUMBLED DRIED ROSEMARY

1/4 CUP CHOPPED FRESH ITALIAN PARSLEY

3 TABLESPOONS TOMATO PASTE

THE LEFTOVER COOKED BONES FROM A PORK, VEAL, OR
BEEF ROAST (AT LEAST 3 TO 4 POUNDS ROASTED
BONE[S])

5 CUPS CANNED, CRUSHED PLUM TOMATOES

3/4 TEASPOON SALT

1/2 CUP GOOD-QUALITY DRY RED WINE

FRESHLY MILLED BLACK OR WHITE PEPPER TO TASTE

In a Dutch oven or large saucepan over medium-low heat, warm the olive oil. Add the carrots, celery, onions, garlic, rosemary, and parsley. Sauté, stirring frequently, until the vegetables are softened, 15 to 20 minutes. Add the tomato paste, using a wooden spoon to distribute it evenly through the vegetables. Add the meat bones, crushed tomatoes, and salt and stir. Cover partially and simmer over medium-low heat for 1 hour, stirring in the wine during the last 20 minutes. Stir the sauce occasionally while it simmers.

Add the pepper and check for salt. When the sauce is finished, it should be thick and thoroughly infused with the flavor of the bones. Remove the bones from the sauce. If there is any meat on them, remove it, chop it, and add it to the sauce.

YIELD: Makes approximately 4 1/2 cups. Two cups are sufficient for saucing 1 pound of pasta.

AHEAD-OF-TIME NOTE: This sauce can be made 4 or 5 days in advance of using and stored tightly covered in the refrigerator, or it can be frozen for up to 3 months.

CHAPTER FIVE

Salse di pomodoro con frutti di mare
Tomato Sauces with Seafood

Salsa di pomodoro e calamari
TOMATO SAUCE WITH SQUID

Salsa di pomodoro e tonno
TOMATO SAUCE WITH TUNA

Salsa di pomodoro con baccalà e olive
TOMATO SAUCE WITH SALT COD AND GREEN OLIVES

Salsa di pomodoro e cozze
TOMATO SAUCE WITH MUSSELS

Salsa di pomodoro e granchi all'Amendolara
ANNA AMENDOLARA'S TOMATO AND CRAB SAUCE

Salsa di pomodoro alla marinara con pesce
TOMATO SAUCE WITH MIXED SEAFOOD

Salsa di pomodoro e vongole
TOMATO SAUCE WITH CLAMS

Salsa di pomodoro e aragosta
TOMATO SAUCE WITH LOBSTER

Salsa di pomodoro e scampi alla sarda
SARDINIAN FRESH TOMATO AND SHRIMP SAUCE

Perhaps the most felicitous of all sauces are those that bring together tomatoes and seafood. The sweetness and acidity of the tomatoes have a natural attraction for the briny character of fish and shellfish alike.

I have talked about the importance of not overcooking tomato sauces except those that contain meat, which may simmer at the gentlest bubble for quite long periods. If ever the maxim for keeping it short applied, it is here, because not only would the clear, sweet tomato taste be lost, but the fish would overcook. The only sauces that simmer longer than twenty or so minutes are those that contain lobster or crab, which require longer cooking due to their shells.

There are not only fresh fish and shellfish dishes in this chapter, but uncommon recipes for making tomato sauces with *baccalà* (salt cod) and with canned tuna, both of which I highly recommend.

Because seafood sauces do not keep or freeze well, I have not included make-ahead instructions in this chapter (exceptions are the sauces made with canned tuna and with *baccalà*, as these fish are both precooked). It should also be noted that seafood sauces are never served with grated cheese.

Salsa di pomodoro e calamari
TOMATO SAUCE WITH SQUID

Squid and tomatoes have a natural affinity for each other. In this simple, flavorful sauce, tomato paste is used rather than tomatoes. Of course, it is a natural with spaghetti, but also delectable folded into a simple *risotto*.

1¼ POUNDS FRESH OR THAWED, FROZEN SQUID

3 TABLESPOONS EXTRA-VIRGIN OLIVE OIL

3 LARGE CLOVES GARLIC, MINCED

⅓ CUP GOOD-QUALITY DRY RED WINE

¾ CUP TOMATO PASTE

1 CUP WATER

¼ TEASPOON SALT

1 TABLESPOON FINELY CHOPPED FRESH ITALIAN PARSLEY

¼ TEASPOON FRESHLY MILLED BLACK PEPPER

Clean the squid according to directions in the recipe for Tomato with Mixed Seafood (page 118), slicing the body into ¼ inch-wide rings. The cleaned tentacles should also be included in this sauce. Make sure to dry the squid thoroughly. This is important, for the excess water will cause the sauce to be thin.

Combine the olive oil and garlic in a cold saucepan. Place over medium-low heat and sauté gently for 1 minute. Then raise the heat to high and immediately add the squid. Sauté over high heat until the squid is seared on all sides, about 5 minutes, tossing constantly to ensure even cooking.

Add the wine, tomato paste, and water. Sauté, stirring to dissolve the tomato paste. Stir in the salt and reduce the heat to low; allow the sauce to simmer for 10 minutes. Add the parsley and simmer for another 10 minutes. Add the pepper, check for seasoning, and remove from the heat. Do not serve with grated cheese.

YIELD: Makes approximately 2½ cups. Two cups are sufficient for saucing 1 pound of pasta.

Salsa di pomodoro e tonno
TOMATO SAUCE WITH TUNA

Italians use canned tuna preserved in olive oil for many sauces, including those containing tomatoes. The combination produces a first-rate sauce for spaghetti or *linguine*. It is also good with egg dishes.

2½ CUPS CANNED, PEELED PLUM TOMATOES IN PURÉE, OR 2½ CUPS CANNED, CRUSHED PLUM TOMATOES PLUS 2 TABLESPOONS TOMATO PASTE

3 TABLESPOONS EXTRA-VIRGIN OLIVE OIL

3 LARGE CLOVES GARLIC, MINCED OR GRATED

½ CUP WATER

½ TEASPOON SALT

PINCH OF RED PEPPER FLAKES

1 TEASPOON CHOPPED FRESH OREGANO, OR ½ TEA-SPOON CRUMBLED DRIED OREGANO

1 CAN (6½ OUNCES) ITALIAN TUNA IN OLIVE OIL, DRAINED AND FINELY FLAKED

If using tomatoes in purée, drain them, reserving the purée. Strain the captured purée to hold back the seeds. Using your fingers, push out the excess seeds from each tomato. Put the tomatoes and the strained purée, or the crushed tomatoes and tomato paste, if you are using them, in a blender. Engage the blender for a few seconds to purée, then set aside.

In a saucepan over medium-low heat, warm the olive oil. Add the garlic and sauté until it softens but does not color, 3 to 4 minutes. Add the puréed tomatoes to the saucepan and stir in the water. Add the salt, red pepper flakes, oregano, and tuna. Cover partially and simmer gently until the sauce is thickened, about 20 minutes. Do not serve with grated cheese.

YIELD: Makes approximately 3 cups. Two cups are sufficient for saucing 1 pound of pasta.

AHEAD-OF-TIME NOTE: This sauce can be made up to 4 days in advance of using and stored tightly covered in the refrigerator, or it can be frozen for up to 3 months.

Salsa di pomodoro con baccalà e olive

TOMATO SAUCE WITH SALT COD AND GREEN OLIVES

Baccalà, dried salt cod, is a staple in many of the coastal regions of Italy, as well as other Mediterranean cuisines. It is simple to prepare once it has been soaked and rehydrated in boiling water. Select fillets that have been skinned and boned before drying; otherwise cleaning the fish is extremely tedious. Use only meaty, light fillets; avoid scrawny, dark pieces. *Baccalà* is found in many ethnic markets in America, including those in Portuguese, Caribbean, and Latin communities. In recent years, I have found it in supermarkets as well.

A tomato and *baccalà* sauce for pasta is typical of southern Italy, where it is served as one of the seven courses in the traditional Christmas Eve fish feast. This is my mother's recipe, and I love the combination of green olives and *baccalà*, despite the fact that both are "salty" foods. Actually, when properly soaked and rehydrated, *baccalà* loses virtually all of its saltiness, but acquires an almost smoky flavor and pleasant, slightly chewy texture. This sauce is lovely with *polenta*, mashed potatoes, or spaghetti or *linguine*.

1 POUND SALT COD FILLET

THICK APPLE SLICE OR 1/2 POTATO

3 TABLESPOONS EXTRA-VIRGIN OLIVE OIL

2 CLOVES GARLIC, MINCED

1 MEDIUM-SIZED YELLOW ONION, MINCED

2 1/2 CUPS CANNED, CRUSHED PLUM TOMATOES

2 TABLESPOONS PITTED AND SLICED, SHARPLY FLAVORED
    IMPORTED GREEN OLIVES SUCH AS PICHOLINE OR
    SICILIAN

1 TABLESPOON RED WINE VINEGAR

2 TABLESPOONS CHOPPED FRESH ITALIAN PARSLEY

1/4 TEASPOON FRESHLY MILLED WHITE OR BLACK
    PEPPER

To prepare the salt cod, place in a bowl with cold water to cover. Add the apple slice or potato half to help draw out the salt. Place in the refrigerator or in a cool place overnight, changing the water several times during the soaking.

Drain the fish and rinse thoroughly in fresh cool water. Remove any errant skin and bones and place the fish in a pot. Add water to cover and place over medium heat. Bring to a boil and cook until the fish is tender, which may take from 20 to 40 minutes. When cooked, the salt cod should be tender and flake easily; it should not be distinegrated or bland. Taste the fish. If it is still excessively salty, drain and cover with plenty of fresh cold water. Bring to a boil once again and test once more. When the fish is ready, drain it, rinse in cold water, and then flake it. Check again for any bones, removing them with your fingers or tweezers. Set aside.

In a saucepan over medium-low heat, warm the olive oil. Add the garlic and onion and sauté until softened, 4 to 5 minutes. Add the tomatoes, olives, vinegar, and 1 tablespoon of the parsley and stir well. Bring to a boil and add the fish. Reduce the heat to medium-low and simmer gently, uncovered, until the sauce thickens, about 20 minutes. Stir the sauce occasionally as it cooks.

Add the remaining 1 tablespoon parsley and the pepper and remove from the heat. Do not serve with grated cheese.

YIELD: Makes approximately 4 cups. Two cups are sufficient for saucing 1 pound of pasta.

AHEAD-OF-TIME NOTE: This sauce can be made up to 4 days in advance of using and stored tightly covered in the refrigerator, or it can be frozen for up to 3 months.

Salsa di pomodoro e cozze
TOMATO SAUCE WITH MUSSELS

As with clam sauce (page 121) the only suitable pasta cuts for this *salsa* are spaghetti or *linguine*.

4 POUNDS SMALL, PLUMP LIVE MUSSELS
SALT
HANDFUL OF CORNMEAL OR FLOUR
3/4 CUP TOMATO PASTE; 1 CUP CANNED, PEELED PLUM
   TOMATOES IN JUICE PLUS 1 TABLESPOON TOMATO
   PASTE; OR 1 POUND FRESH, SWEET, MATURE VINE-
   RIPENED TOMATOES PLUS 1 TABLESPOON TOMATO
   PASTE
4 TABLESPOONS EXTRA-VIRGIN OLIVE OIL
2 CLOVES GARLIC, UNPEELED, AND 2 LARGE CLOVES,
   CHOPPED
1/4 TEASPOON SALT, OR TO TASTE
FRESHLY MILLED BLACK PEPPER TO TASTE
1 TABLESPOON CHOPPED FRESH ITALIAN PARSLEY

Using a stiff brush, scrub the mussels vigorously and remove all the beards. If they are very sandy, place them in a bowl of cool water with a few big pinches of salt and the cornmeal or flour. Place in the refrigerator for at least 3 hours or as long as overnight so that they will purge themselves of the sand. Then drain, scrub again, and rinse well in cool running water. Set aside in the refrigerator.

If using only tomato paste, set aside. If using canned tomatoes, drain them, reserving their juice for another use. Using your fingers, push out the excess seeds from each tomato. Chop the tomatoes and set aside with the 1 tablespoon of tomato paste. If using fresh tomatoes, slip them into a saucepan of

rapidly boiling water and blanch for 30 to 45 seconds. Drain the tomatoes and immediately plunge them into cold water. Drain again and, using a paring knife, lift off the skins and cut out the tough core portions. Cut into quarters lengthwise and, using your fingers, push out the excess seeds. Chop the tomatoes and place in a colander to drain for 5 minutes. Set aside with the 1 tablespoon of tomato paste.

Put 1 tablespoon of the olive oil, the unpeeled whole garlic cloves, and the mussels in a large, heavy pot and cover tightly. (Leaving the skins on the garlic cloves will prevent them from browning and thus imparting a bitter flavor to the sauce.) Place the pot over high heat and toss the mussels now and then to ensure equal exposure to the heat. As soon as the mussels open (about 6 minutes), remove from the heat and allow to cool in the pot. When they are cool enough to handle, remove the mussels from their shells with a small knife, allowing the liquid in the shell to run into the pot. Discard the shells. Strain all the liquid in the pan through a sieve lined with cheesecloth (or a paper towel) to remove any sand, capturing the liquid in a clean bowl. Discard the garlic. Put the mussels back in their liquid and set aside.

In a cold saucepan over medium-low heat, warm the remaining 3 tablespoons olive oil with the chopped garlic. Sauté until the garlic is soft, 3 to 4 minutes. Then add the tomato paste, or the chopped drained tomatoes plus 1 tablespoon paste. Stir well and season with the salt and pepper. Add 1/2 cup of the strained mussel juice (reserve the remaining juice for another use) and simmer, uncovered, over low heat until the sauce thickens, 10 to 15 minutes. Raise the heat to medium and as soon as the sauce starts to boil, turn off the heat. Check for seasoning and strew with the parsley. Do not pass grated cheese.

YIELD: Makes approximately 2 cups. This recipe is sufficient for saucing 1 pound of pasta.

Salsa di pomodoro e granchi all'Amendolara
ANNA AMENDOLARA'S TOMATO AND CRAB SAUCE

This delicious sauce is served with dried pasta—*linguine* or spaghetti—and the crabs are offered as a second course.

12 HARD-SHELL BLUE CRABS, PREFERABLY FEMALE
5 CUPS CANNED, PEELED PLUM TOMATOES IN PURÉE
¾ CUP EXTRA-VIRGIN OLIVE OIL
4 LARGE CLOVES GARLIC, BRUISED
2 TEASPOONS CHOPPED FRESH OREGANO, OR 1 TEA-
   SPOON CRUMBLED DRIED OREGANO
½ CUP CHOPPED FRESH ITALIAN PARSLEY
SALT TO TASTE
2 SMALL DRIED HOT RED PEPPERS (OPTIONAL)

Have the fishmonger remove the top shell from each crab for easier handling. Turn each crab on its back and pull the apron (flap) up and off. Remove the spongy white gills, which are inedible. Twist off the swimmerettes, which are the back fins, and rinse the crabs under cold running water. Working over a bowl to catch any juices from the crabs, snap each crab body in half lengthwise. Set aside.

Drain the tomatoes, reserving the purée. Strain the captured purée to hold back the seeds. Using your fingers, push out the excess seeds from each tomato. Chop the tomatoes and set aside with the purée.

In a wide, deep skillet large enough to hold the crabs eventually, warm the olive oil over medium-low heat. Add the garlic and cook, stirring occasionally, until golden, 1 or 2 minutes. Add the crabs and stir often until they color (the underside will become opaque; the claws will turn red), about 10 minutes. Add the tomatoes and purée, oregano, parsley, salt, and the hot peppers, if using. Cover partially and adjust the heat to maintain a gentle simmer. Cook until the sauce has thickened slightly, about 30 minutes. Do not serve the sauce with grated cheese.

YIELD: Makes approximately 4 cups. This is sufficient for saucing 1 pound of pasta.

Salsa di pomodoro alla marinara con pesce
TOMATO SAUCE WITH MIXED SEAFOOD

Versions of this sauce appear all along Italy's coastline, where fresh seafood is abundant. Many varieties of fish and shellfish can be used, but it is best to stick to firm-fleshed white fish that won't fall apart in the sauce. Delicate fish such as sole and flounder are not appropriate. It is very important not to overcook the fish and, above all, it should be impeccably fresh.

Instructions for cleaning squid follow, although if your fishmonger will clean the squid for you, so much the better. Tell him or her to cut the body into ¼-inch-wide rings and to include the cleaned tentacles. Buy only young, small squid; avoid large, tough ones. Adding the salt *after* the squid is cooked will keep it tender.

While the most popular purpose for this sauce is to serve it with either *linguine* or spaghetti, it can be eaten simply with thick slices of crusty Italian or French bread, toasted or not. Drizzle the bread or toast with a little extra-virgin olive oil before dunking.

1 DOZEN SMALLEST LIVE LITTLENECK CLAMS, 1 POUND
   LIVE THUMB-SIZED WEST COAST CLAMS OR COCKLES,
   OR 1 POUND LIVE MEDIUM MUSSELS
SALT
HANDFUL OF CORNMEAL OR FLOUR
1¼ POUNDS FRESH OR THAWED, FROZEN SQUID
1 POUND FIRM, WHITE-FLESHED FISH FILLETS SUCH
   AS COD, HADDOCK, HALIBUT, OR TURBOT, CUT INTO
   2-INCH-WIDE STRIPS
½ POUND SHRIMP, PEELED AND DEVEINED
2 CUPS CANNED, PEELED PLUM TOMATOES IN JUICE,
   OR 2 POUNDS FRESH, SWEET, MATURE VINE-RIPENED
   TOMATOES
¼ CUP EXTRA-VIRGIN OLIVE OIL
2 LARGE CLOVES GARLIC, MINCED
1 SMALL YELLOW ONION, MINCED
4 TABLESPOONS CHOPPED FRESH ITALIAN PARSLEY
2 TABLESPOONS TOMATO PASTE
½ CUP GOOD-QUALITY DRY WHITE WINE

1 TEASPOON CHOPPED FRESH OREGANO, OR ½
   TEASPOON CRUMBLED DRIED OREGANO
⅛ TEASPOON RED PEPPER FLAKES
1 TEASPOON SALT

Using a stiff brush, scrub the clams or mussels well; if using mussels, remove their beards. Place the clams or mussels in a bowl of cool water with a few big pinches of salt and the cornmeal or flour. Place in the refrigerator for at least 3 hours or as long as overnight so that the shellfish will purge themselves of sand. Then drain, scrub again, and rinse well in cool running water.

To clean the squid, holding the body (sac) in one hand and the tentacle end in the other, pull them apart. The two parts will separate easily. Using scissors or a knife, cut off the tentacles just above the eyes; discard everything below the eyes. Use your fingers to push out the small, bony "beak" at

the base of the tentacles. Pull out the cellophane-like "spine" from the body and discard it. Peel off the speckled skin. Rinse the squid well in cool running water. Cut the body into ¼-inch-wide rings. Leave the tentacles whole unless they are particularly large; if they are, cut them in half.

Thoroughly pat the clams, mussels, squid, fish fillet strips and peeled shrimp dry. Refrigerate until needed.

If using canned tomatoes, drain them, reserving their juice for another use. Using your fingers, push out the excess seeds from each tomato. Chop the tomatoes and set aside. If using fresh tomatoes, slip them into a saucepan of rapidly boiling water and blanch for 30 to 45 seconds. Drain the tomatoes and immediately plunge them into cold water. Drain again and, using a paring knife, lift off the skins and cut out the tough core portions. Cut into quarters lengthwise and, using your fingers, push out the excess seeds. Chop the tomatoes and place in a colander to drain for 5 minutes.

In a large skillet or Dutch oven over medium heat, warm the olive oil. Add the garlic and onion and sauté for 3 to 4 minutes. Add 2 tablespoons of the parsley and continue to sauté until the vegetables soften but do not color, about 7 minutes. Add the tomato paste and wine and continue to cook, stirring, until the alcohol evaporates, about 3 minutes.

Add the tomatoes, oregano, and red pepper flakes and simmer over medium-low heat for 5 minutes. Increase the heat to high and add the squid; sauté for 5 minutes, tossing frequently to ensure even cooking. Add the salt, the clams or mussels, strips of fish fillet, and shrimp and stir to expose all of the seafood to the heat of the pan. Cook until the mollusks open, 8 to 10 minutes.

Stir in the remaining 2 tablespoons parsley and remove from the heat. Do not serve this sauce with grated cheese.

YIELD: Makes approximately 2 cups. This recipe is sufficient for saucing 1 pound of pasta.

Salsa di pomodoro e vongole
TOMATO SAUCE WITH CLAMS

The only pasta cuts suitable here are spaghetti or *linguine*. As simple as this sauce is, there are many ways to use one of the basic sauces as a starting point.

3 DOZEN SMALLEST LIVE LITTLENECK CLAMS, OR 3
   POUNDS LIVE THUMB-SIZED WEST COAST CLAMS
1 RECIPE RUSTIC TOMATO SAUCE (PAGE 46) OR LIGHT
   PURÉED FRESH TOMATO SAUCE (PAGE 42)
SALT
HANDFUL OF CORNMEAL OR FLOUR
2 TABLESPOONS EXTRA-VIRGIN OLIVE OIL
2 LARGE CLOVES GARLIC, MINCED
2 TABLESPOONS CHOPPED FRESH ITALIAN PARSLEY
SMALL PINCH OF RED PEPPER FLAKES, OR TO TASTE

Using a stiff brush, scrub the clams well and place them in a bowl of cool water with a few big pinches of salt and the cornmeal or flour. Place in the refrigerator for at least 3 hours or as long as overnight so that the clams will purge themselves of sand.

Make the sauce. While it cooks, drain and scrub the clams again and then rinse them well in cool running water; drain well, pat dry, and set aside in the refrigerator.

In a large, cold skillet, combine the olive oil, garlic, 1 tablespoon of the parsley, and the red pepper flakes. Sauté over medium-low heat until the garlic softens but does not color, 3 to 4 minutes. Add the tomato sauce and heat through, stirring occasionally, about 8 minutes.

Raise the heat to medium, add the clams, cover, and cook until the clams open, 8 to 10 minutes. Remove from the heat and stir in the remaining 1 tablespoon of parsley. The shells can be left in the sauce, or if you prefer, remove some of the clams from their shells, return them to the sauce, and discard the empty shells. Do not serve with grated cheese.

YIELD: Makes approximately 2 cups. This recipe is sufficient for saucing 1 pound of pasta.

Salsa di pomodoro e aragosta
TOMATO SAUCE WITH LOBSTER

Saffron is often married with seafood sauces in Sardinia. It imparts the subtlest flavor and an intense red tint. Lobster, even more than other seafoods, has a particular affinity to saffron. This recipe should be served with spaghetti or *linguine*.

2 RECIPES NEAPOLITAN TOMATO SAUCE (PAGE 47), OR RUSTIC TOMATO SAUCE (PAGE 46)
3 TABLESPOONS EXTRA-VIRGIN OLIVE OIL
4 LARGE CLOVES GARLIC, MINCED
2 LIVE LOBSTERS, 1¼ POUNDS EACH
4 ENVELOPES (¼ TEASPOON TOTAL) SAFFRON POWDER, OR ½ TEASPOON SAFFRON THREADS
FRESHLY MILLED BLACK PEPPER TO TASTE

Make the sauce and set aside.

Rinse the lobsters in cold water. Split them in half lengthwise and pull out the black vein that runs the length of the body. Remove the tiny sand sac near the base of the head. Cut each in half again; crack the claws; rinse in cold running water. (If you prefer, you can have your fishmonger do this, but the lobsters should be cooked soon after they are butchered.) Set aside.

In a Dutch oven or other wide pan large enough to hold the lobsters eventually, heat the olive oil and garlic together over medium-low heat. Sauté gently until the garlic softens but does not color, about 1 minute. Add the lobsters. Stir often until they turn red, turning them to cook evenly, about 6 minutes.

Add the sauce to the pan. If using saffron threads, heat them gently in a small pan on the stove top for 1 minute. Then crush them between your fingers and stir them into the sauce. If using saffron powder, simply stir it into the sauce. Cover partially and simmer over medium heat, stirring frequently, until the lobsters are thoroughly cooked, about 20 minutes.

When the lobsters are ready, add the pepper and serve at once. Do not pass grated cheese.

YIELD: Makes approximately 4 cups. Two cups are sufficient for saucing 1 pound of pasta.

Salsa di pomodoro e scampi alla sarda
SARDINIAN FRESH TOMATO AND SHRIMP SAUCE

Here is a Sardinian sauce that requires very little work, but produces very tasty results. The combination of the onion, the quickly cooked fresh tomatoes that have been strained to remove bitter seeds, and the clear flavor of the shrimp make the sauce startlingly sweet. Fold it into a simple *risotto*, serve it alongside plain white rice, toss it with spaghetti or *linguine*, or just offer it with lots of good, sturdy Italian-style bread.

3 TABLESPOONS EXTRA-VIRGIN OLIVE OIL
1 LARGE YELLOW ONION, CHOPPED
1½ LARGE BAY LEAVES
⅛ TEASPOON RED PEPPER FLAKES
2½ POUNDS FRESH, SWEET, MATURE VINE-RIPENED
   TOMATOES
2 POUNDS SHRIMP, PEELED AND DEVEINED
3 TABLESPOONS CHOPPED FRESH ITALIAN PARSLEY
SALT TO TASTE

In a large skillet over medium heat, warm the olive oil. Add the onion, bay leaves, and red pepper flakes and sauté until the onion is softened but not browned, 5 or 6 minutes. Then place a food mill over the skillet and pass the tomatoes through it, forcing through as much pulp as possible. Stir in the tomatoes well. Cook gently, uncovered, until much of the water from the tomatoes has evaporated, about 50 minutes. The sauce should coat a spoon when it is ready.

Add the shrimp and cook over medium heat until they turn pink and curl, about 8 minutes (the timing will depend on the size of the shrimp; small ones may cook more quickly, while the largest ones may take as long as 10 minutes).

Remove from the heat and stir in the parsley and salt. Do not serve with grated cheese.

YIELD: Makes approximately 4 cups. Two cups are sufficient for saucing 1 pound of pasta.

Mail-Order Sources

AMERICAN SPOON FOODS
P.O. Box 566
Petoskey, Michigan 49770
616/347-9030, 800/222-5886
Dried morels, porcini, *and* shiitakes.

AUX DELICES DES BOIS, INC.
14 Leonard Street
New York, NY 10013
212/334-1230
All types of cultivated and imported mushrooms, sun-dried tomatoes. Will accept phone orders for overnight delivery.

DEAN & DELUCA
Mail-Order Department
560 Broadway
New York, NY 10012
212/431-1691, 800/221-7714, ext 223 or 270
Kitchen equipment; Italian specialty foods, imported dried mushrooms. Catalog available.

G.B. RATTO INTERNATIONAL GROCER
821 Washington Street
Oakland, California 94607
800/228-3515(CA), 800/325-3483(out of state)
Italian specialty foods, imported dried mushrooms, large assortment of grains, flours, herbs and spices. Catalog available.

HANS JOHANSSON
44 West 74th Street
New York, NY, 10023
212/787-6496
Dried morels, porcini, *black trumpets,* chanterelles, *and* shiitakes.

MANGANARO FOODS
488 Ninth Ave.
New York, NY 10018
212/563-5331, 800/472-5264
Italian specialty foods, imported dried mushrooms. Catalog available.

METRO AGRI BUSINESS
47 Wooster Street
New York, NY 10013
212/431-3504
Dried porcini *and morels.*

THE MOZZARELLA COMPANY
2944 Elm Street
Dallas, Texas 75226
214/741-4072, 800/798-2954
Large variety of fresh and aged cheeses; sun-dried tomatoes; imported olive oils and balsamic vinegars. Cheeses shipped overnight.

THE SANDY MUSH HERB NURSERY
Route 2, Surrett Cove Road
Leicester, North Carolina 28748
704/683-2014
Live herbs and herb seeds shipped. Lovely illustrated catalog ($4, refundable with first order) includes suggested herb-garden patterns, information about growing and drying herbs, and recipes.

SHEPHERD'S GARDEN SEEDS
Shipping Office
30 Irene Street
Torrington, Connecticut 06790
203/482-3638
Large selection of seeds for vegetables, herbs, and flowers. Catalog available.

TODARO BROTHERS
555 Second Avenue
New York, NY 10016
212/679-7766
Italian specialty foods, imported cheeses. Catalog available.

VIVANDE PORTA VIA
2125 Fillmore Street
San Francisco, California 94115
415/346-4430
Imported seeds for hard-to-find Italian vegetable varieties; Italian specialty foods.

WILLIAMS-SONOMA
Mail-Order Department
P.O. Box 7456
San Francisco, California 94120-7456
415/421-4242, 800/541-2233
Kitchen equipment; some Italian specialty foods. Catalog available.

W.J. CLARK & CO.
5400 West Roosevelt Road
Chicago, Illinois 60650
312/626-3676, 800/229-0090
Dried porcini, shiitakes, morels, and oyster mushrooms; chopped and powdered, dried wild mushrooms. Catalog available.

ZABAR'S
Mail-Order Department
2245 Broadway
New York, NY 10024
212/787-2003, 800/221-3347
Kitchen equipment; some Italian specialty foods, imported cheeses. Catalog available.

Index

Table of Equivalents

THE EXACT EQUIVALENTS IN THE
FOLLOWING TABLES HAVE BEEN
ROUNDED FOR CONVENIENCE.

US/UK	METRIC
oz=ounce	g=gram
lb=pound	kg=kilogram
in=inch	mm=millimeter
ft=foot	cm=centimeter
tbl=tablespoon	ml=milliliter
fl oz=fluid ounce	l=liter
qt=quart	

Weights

US/UK	METRIC
1 oz	30 g
2 oz	60 g
3 oz	90 g
4 oz (¼ lb)	125 g
5 oz (⅓ lb)	155 g
6 oz	185 g
7 oz	220 g
8 oz (½ lb)	250 g
10 oz	315 g
12 oz (¾ lb)	375 g
14 oz	440 g
16 oz (1 lb)	500 g
1½ lb	750 g
2 lb	1 kg
3 lb	1.5 kg

Oven Temperatures

FAHRENHEIT	CELSIUS	GAS
250	120	½
275	140	1
300	150	2
325	160	3
350	180	4
375	190	5
400	200	6
425	220	7
450	230	8
475	240	9
500	260	10

Liquids

US	METRIC	UK
2 tbl	30 ml	1 fl oz
¼ cup	60 ml	2 fl oz
⅓ cup	80 ml	3 fl oz
½ cup	125 ml	4 fl oz
⅔ cup	160 ml	5 fl oz
¾ cup	180 ml	6 fl oz
1 cup	250 ml	8 fl oz
1½ cups	375 ml	12 fl oz
2 cups	500 ml	16 fl oz
4 cups/1 qt	1 liter	32 fl oz

Length Measures

⅛ in	3 mm
¼ in	6 mm
½ in	12 mm
1 in	2.5 cm
2 in	5 cm
3 in	7.5 cm
4 in	10 cm
5 in	13 cm
6 in	15 cm
7 in	18 cm
8 in	20 cm
9 in	23 cm
10 in	25 cm
11 in	28 cm
12 in/1 ft	30 cm

EQUIVALENTS FOR COMMONLY USED INGREDIENTS

Long-Grain Rice

⅓ cup	2 oz	60 g
½ cup	2½ oz	75 g
¾ cup	4 oz	125 g
1 cup	5 oz	155 g
1½ cups	8 oz	250 g

All-Purpose Flour/Dried Bread Crumbs

¼ cup	1 oz	30 g
⅓ cup	1½ oz	45 g
½ cup	2 oz	60 g
¾ cup	3 oz	90 g
1 cup	4 oz	125 g
1½ cups	6 oz	185 g
2 cups	8 oz	250 g

Grated Parmesan/Romano Cheese

¼ cup	1 oz	30 g
½ cup	2 oz	60 g
¾ cup	3 oz	90 g
1 cup	4 oz	125 g
1⅓ cups	5 oz	155 g
2 cups	7 oz	220 g